This Ol'
Drought
Ain't Broke Us
Yet

This Ol' Drought Ain't Broke Us Yet

Stories from the American West

Jim Garry

Mother,
— I bought this
for you at Hubbard
Museum at Riodoso —
July 10, 2004 —
Love,
Jane

JOHNSON BOOKS
Boulder

Published in the United States by Johnson Books, a Division of Johnson Publishing Company, 1880 South 57th Court, Boulder, Colorado 80301. Originally published in hardcover as part of the Library of the American West, Herman J. Viola, editor, by Crown Publishers, a division of Random House, Inc.

9   8   7   6   5   4   3   2   1

Library of Congress Cataloging-in-Publication Data
Garry, Jim.
    This ol' drought ain't broke us yet :
stories from the American West / Jim Garry.—1st ed.
        p.   cm.
    1. West (U.S.)—Social life and customs—Anecdotes.
2. Folklore—West (U.S.)—I. Title. II. Series.
F596.G38   1992
978—dc20   92-12629
                                                                                CIP

ISBN 1-55566-170-X

Printed in the United States by
Johnson Printing
1880 South 57th Court
Boulder, Colorado 80301

 Printed on recycled paper with soy ink

To my parents, Momma and Daddy,
who gave me my first stories.

Contents

Acknowledgments

There is no way to thank everyone who has contributed to a book like this. Some of these stories I've known so long that I can't even remember where I first heard them, let alone who told them to me. I've tried to acknowledge the source of each story, when I know it; when the person doesn't mind his name being used; and when the statute of limitations has run out. But there are some special people who have made the book possible.

Herman Viola has encouraged and helped me for years; indeed, he's the one who introduced me to the publishing world and made it possible for me to try to translate some of my oral material into written form. My sister, Grace Mary, who has also encouraged me to write for years, probably regretted it when I did, because I turned her into an editor. Without her help, this book would never have approached a literary form. Earl and Ethel Throne graciously provided me with a place to work, a place at the far end of several miles of bad road so that I was able to work without interruptions. Steve Topping, my editor, showed a great deal of patience when I know he didn't really feel it. The folks at Sheridan Office Services, Shari Peddicord, Cathy

Samuelson, and Jill Whaples, did yeoman service in getting the manuscript typed into a legible format. I want to thank Sandy Nykerk for the picture that makes me look considerably better than I do.

The people I want most to acknowledge, to thank, are all the people over the last forty-odd years who have told me stories, sharing their lives and their histories with me. For each story told there are dozens, seldom if ever repeated, that form the foundation I work from. To everyone, named and nameless, I can only say thank you.

This Ol'
Drought
Ain't Broke Us
Yet

SEARCHING
FOR THE
YEGUA KNOBS

.∧.∧.∧.∧.∧.

In the summer of 1916, Uncle Emzy bought some cattle, range delivered, down on Yegua Creek in the Post Oaks, twenty miles below our place. The Post Oaks of Central Texas are the western edge of the Great American Forest. There was a time, so the stories run, when a squirrel could travel from there to the Atlantic Ocean without touching the ground, simply moving through the treetops. The Post Oaks, as befitted a forest edge, broke out from solid forest into a savanna of cedar, post oak, and live oak stands separated by prairie. The western edge of the Old South, it was settled by old Anglo-Saxon stock that produced large families, small farms, and the type of pride and short temper that resulted in feuds. After it became thoroughly fenced and people started suppressing wildfires, the trees and brush spread and the grasslands shrank. But in 1916, when Uncle Emzy bought the cattle, the Post Oaks were closer, ecologically and socially, to 1850 than to 1950. For that matter the Post Oaks were more like 1850 than 1950 *in* 1950. Yegua Creek heads in springs on the Yegua Knobs, three rounded, tree-covered hills joined by a pair of low saddles. The Knobs are the dominant feature in that part of the country.

Daddy was twelve that summer and ready to learn what Uncle Emzy had to teach about horses and horsemanship. So Daddy worked for Uncle Emzy all summer and was paid in knowledge, which was considerably more valuable to Daddy in the long run. Besides, money was, for Uncle Emzy, in considerably shorter supply in the short run.

The day they went to gather the cattle on Yegua Creek, Daddy, with the curiosity of a twelve-year-old who had grown up in flat country, wanted to get to the top of the Knobs to see the view. But the cattle were around the base, giving Daddy neither an excuse nor the leisure to go to the top of them. As they drove the cattle home, Daddy promised himself that, someday, he would get to the top of the Yegua Knobs.

If you aren't familiar with places like the Post Oaks, you might think that such a promise would be easily kept. Not so. Post Oakers were a clannish people, which is the main reason the twentieth century made such slow inroads in that part of the world. Even today, many of the roads are sand, occasionally axle-deep, and most folks, when they talk at all, tell stories rather than give directions. If you couple those two facts with the third fact that the country is thick enough with trees and brush to be hard to see where you or anything else is, you have the makings of family mythology; Daddy has been trying to get to the top of the Yegua Knobs for better than seventy-five years.

When Buz and Grace Mary, my brother and sister, and I were little, Sunday-afternoon drives often were aimed at the Knobs, but of course never arrived. As we grew older, and the Sunday-afternoon expeditions continued, I came to realize that the Yegua Knobs were no normal hills. We would spot them in the distance and start toward them. Trees would screen them from our view, and though the road ran straight, when the Knobs reappeared they would still be on the horizon but now off to the right or left, or even behind us. As we grew still older and traveled more widely, we laughed at every set of three peaks, hills, or bumps on the horizon and called them the Yegua Knobs. Over time they came to signify, for me, that goal on the horizon that must be striven for, but is never to be attained. The Yegua Knobs are, no matter where I am, there on the horizon, teasing me on. They are not simply earth, rock, vegetation, and mockingbirds, but are composed equally of mystic qualities, principles, ideas, and ideals. And they are never fixed in place. Wherever I stand, they are on the horizon, beckoning me on. For they are the unattainable lessons that shape our lives. For me, the lessons the Knobs have sent me after are lessons of the land.

The lessons have always come to me as stories. Originally, of course, I had no idea that I was collecting stories; I was just listening—sometimes because I wanted to hear the tales, sometimes because I couldn't escape. When I was really little, my great-grandmother, Mamoish, often visited, and I can remember her sitting me down and telling the story of the Yankees coming to her parents' plantation in Alabama. Her father was gone to the War and her mother was running the place, a horse farm, in his absence. She told of watching the Yankee cavalry taking all their brood mares as replacement mounts, but leaving the foals, still too young to wean, since they couldn't keep up. One of the slaves, who had openly talked of clearing out and going north to freedom when the Yankees arrived, took off with the troops. A day or two later he returned, with all the brood mares he'd stolen back from the Yankees. He worked for the family the rest of his life. The significance of the story to Mamoish—and through her to me—was that the man would, the rest of his life, never have anything to do with Yankees. Any people who would treat horses like that, taking mares and leaving their foals to starve, were not people he would have any dealings with.

The stories I heard as a child, listening to my kinfolks, were better than those on the radio and television. They were the stories of the first Texians and the world they built. They were the stories of warfare, of adventure, of wild horses and cattle, of badmen and lawmen, and of the simple ways of the early settlers. They were the stories of farmers and cotton buyers, of the railroad and the growth of our town. They were the stories of black farm workers on our place, one of whom was old enough to remember the first Juneteenth, the day word of the Emancipation Proclamation reached Texas. They were the stories of vaqueros, told by one grown old, who worked for us. And there were books, a house full of them, filled with stories of the old days and the old ways.

Daddy's mother's—my Gram Ada's—family had come to Texas when it was still part of Mexico, and had moved out onto the "Wild Horse Prairies" when, as the old-timers said, dirt was still new in the country. Her husband, my grandfather, who died before my time, came with his parents when they built the first cotton compress. Mother's family, the Murphys, built the railroad to Taylor and stayed on to build and run two hotels. The stories I grew up on were the history of that land and, by implication, the history of all land and the people who love it. For instance, Gram Ada's birthday parties, on January first, were storytelling sessions of the first order. Gram Ada had nieces and nephews older than she was and plenty of cousins around her age—old. The stories varied from long, lean Frate's dry, deadpan, but utterly hilarious tales to Anno's acting out each story as she told it. Through the afternoon, each story was better than the one before it. I was learning the first rule of storytelling: "The first liar never has a chance."

Pop, Mamma's father, was the police chief in Taylor when I was little. He had been the police chief for so long that everyone in town called him Chief, even after he retired. He had more than a few stories of the sort that enthrall small boys. His son, my uncle James, had worked for Brown and Root, then one of the world's largest construction firms, in its early days and told me tales of building roads in the horse-and-mule days as well as the switch to modern equipment and forming his own company. Mother had taught in country schools during the Depression and was full of stories of the Germans and Czechs who had settled on small farms on the creeks around us, and of their children's attempts to learn the language as well as their lessons.

Especially, though, there was Daddy, the best of the storytellers, the best of the historians, the best of the rememberers. He provided the warp that all the yarns were woven through. He knew all the stories and their contexts. He had a story for every lesson, a story for every occasion. And for him the Yegua Knobs had never moved, they were right there, just over his horizon; all his stories were grown from or adapted to that piece of earth he had always called home.

I was surrounded with told stories, not just local ones but folktales from Ireland, England, Central Europe, Africa, and Mexico. There were writers like Mark Twain, J. Frank Dobie, and Joel Chandler Harris who fueled my love of the spoken language that I picked up from the told stories. But the Yegua Knobs were pushing me to hear not just the stories of the people who lived on and loved the land, but the stories of the land itself. When it started raining again, in '57 (we'd had a little drought during the fifties—the biblical seven years. I'd never, to my memory, seen water running in Brushy, the creek that ran through our place, until I was ten years old), Daddy stocked the tanks, reservoirs for stock water, with fish. One of the tanks was only a couple of hundred yards from the house, close enough to reach even if only a few minutes were available. It was there that I first heard, somewhere down on the creek, what I identified years later as the pipes of Pan. There I learned to watch the bullbats soar and dive for bugs, to see the bats come out as the clouds put on their evening show. It was there that I first began to look beyond the distant plains horizon, and wonder what was there and what stories were told. And I knew that just over one horizon were the Yegua Knobs.

As I got older the horizon began to expand, but always on it, though seldom in the same place twice, the Yegua Knobs loomed. For instance, when I left home to go to college, I knew I was woefully unprepared, but I had no idea how unprepared I really was. I stepped off the train in Ann Arbor at midnight, two days from home, and stood alone in the station, nearly paralyzed from culture shock. Paralysis turned into sheer terror the next day, when, forced to eat in a café since the dorms weren't yet opened, I ordered a chicken-fried steak and drew a blank look from the waitress. I was fifteen hundred miles from home and in the land of heathens. The terror increased with each day of orientation. I had never before lived in town. I had never before been around so many people, all of whom seemed to believe they were smart and well educated; I knew I wasn't well educated and doubted I was smart.

The first class I attended, in chemistry, was bigger

than my high school had been. Terror was edging toward panic when, on my second day of classes, I attended my first class at the School of Natural Resources. The class title was Introduction to Field Ecology. Like the vast majority of people in those pre–Earth Day days, I was unfamiliar with the word *ecology*. Traditional peoples understand that one of the most effective ways to teach is first to get the student into a heightened state of awareness. One of the most widely used methods is to terrify the person. When boys are abducted to go through their puberty rites they are ritually killed, the child dying and the man being resurrected. The catch is that no one tells the child that his death is only symbolic. His terror heightens his awareness so that he feels his death and resurrection and knows at a depth far greater than normal what has happened to him, and he is changed: The child is dead and the wonders of the adult world are opened. I was in such a state of terror when I went from the opening lecture of Introduction to Field Ecology to the library. The first thing I did was to break out a dictionary and look up the word. Webster said, "**e-col´-o-gy,** n. [from Gr. *oikos*, house; and -*logy*]." That was followed by a picture of the Yegua Knobs. Suddenly, clearly, I knew the meaning of the word and what would actually be required to understand ecology, to understand not just one room of the house or just the plumbing or electrical system, but the whole house. It would involve not only the biology that I had come to Ann Arbor to study, but history, literature, and art as well as all the other sciences.

I almost folded my hand then, but the fear of failure is a wonderful motivator. I toughed it out through the first year, barely. Then, in my sophomore year, I met the Society of Les Voyageurs, a collection of students and faculty who were professional wilderness nuts. My sanity, if not my grade point average, was saved. For four years I took all the required courses plus auditing all the art history, literature, history, and the like that the Knobs definition of ecology required of me. I also realized that the faculty of the School of Natural Resources used stories to illustrate all important points. There was, it seemed to me, some connection between the land and stories of substance, of endurance.

Between my fourth and fifth years (school wasn't easy, it took a while) in Ann Arbor, I took off to wander around the West, looking at land and listening to stories. The trip started with about six weeks of research with John Turner in the Jackson Hole and Yellowstone country. That was twenty-odd years ago. I'm still in Wyoming. The country grabbed me. The people of the land talked to me. After finishing at Ann Arbor and doing my stint in the army, I stayed at the Turner ranch for several years, learning the land and listening to stories. Then I moved to the Powder River Basin and found, in my travels, the rest of the state.

Always in my travels, no matter what the reason for the trip, the stories have been there. I've always loved listening to them and have always understood that for them to survive they must be passed on; oral tradition is always a single generation away from extinction. I have listened to the stories because they teach me the culture of the place and the important lessons the culture has to teach. In rural America the cultures and hence the stories are shaped by the land, so the lessons are the land's.

For five years I concentrated on learning Wyoming's lands and stories, though I knew they could not be totally separated from other places and other stories. Then, while I was finishing up a two-year Wyoming Arts Council residency as a film and video artist at Sheridan College, Lynne Simpson, a member of the local Arts Council, asked me to tell some of the stories I'd heard while collecting Wyoming folkways as part of my residency. In a small theater in Sheridan, I sat and told stories of Bill Daniels, one of my old mentors in the mountains. Suddenly Bill, six years dead, was sitting there with me, reminding me of the good stories. And I knew that all the years I'd searched for a voice—in film, in poetry, in photography, in essays—had been a foundation for this night. My voice was my voice. All my life I had collected the stories that the Yegua Knobs had led me to. They had been told to me, I was to tell them to others.

Peter Hassrick, the director of the Buffalo Bill Historical Center in Cody, Wyoming, was in the audience that night. The next week, Gene Ball, the educational director at BBHC, called me to see if I would be interested in telling stories there for a couple of weeks that summer. My grant at the college was over, and I knew it was time for me to devote myself to collecting and telling stories. I've been at it for better than a dozen years now, living often on the good graces of many people who feel that preserving the stories is important. What follows are some of the tales I've picked up while searching for the Yegua Knobs. If you don't like the stories, then stay in town, always, for they are largely the stories of the land. If you don't like the way the stories are written, take it out on me, for I've had to translate them from spoken form. If you really want to enjoy the stories, then do as I've done: go out and listen to them. They are there, everywhere around us.

But for now, sit down next to the fire or under a shade tree, listen to the world for a time, and when things have quieted down, open the book and let out the wonderful old-timers to sit with you and tell you their stories. If you can hear them tell the tales, look around you when they're done. Somewhere on the horizon you will see three low hills. Go there.

A MAN ON
FOOT...

⋀⋀⋀⋀⋀

When I was three, I was given Texas, my cousin Jimmie's aging, outgrown Shetland pony. For more than a year I was only allowed to ride in the pony ring, a circular pen Daddy had built for Grace Mary, Buz, and me to learn to ride in. From the first day I rode outside that ring I have looked down on pedestrians. I follow a long and illustrious line, dating back thousands of years. The ancient Greeks were so impressed with the horse tribes to the north that stories of the centaurs entered the Greek myths; Genghis Khan's troops were inheritors of the idea. Knights in Europe were aware of the ascendancy the horse gave them; the aristocratic Arabs of the desert would never think of walking. We polish our shoes because the Spanish dons did so to show that they did not walk. In our own country the cowboy, hero of our myths, rides across the wild, wide western landscape, preferably on a mustang. Every horseman knows that a man on foot is no man at all.

Riding a horse doesn't make you a horseman. No, there's something more, just as two people living together doesn't make a marriage. The relationship between horse and horseman is special and not easily defined, but very obvious when you see it. It has been my privilege to have been around good horsemen, in life and in legend, since birth. I have sought them out to learn about horses and to hear their stories. I'm not sure I know which lessons have taken a better hold.

Grandpa Barker had a slave who was reputed to be one of the best horsemen ever in that part of the country. After the Civil War, he stayed on and worked for the Barkers until Uncle Bob and Uncle Frate were well into their teens and educated as horsemen to his satisfaction. Then he moved to North Texas and worked as the foreman on a large horse ranch. He was so knowledgeable of horses that the rancher took him with him on annual horse-buying trips to the thoroughbred country of Kentucky and Virginia. On one of these trips the foreman bought a thoroughbred stallion and sent it to Uncle Bob and Uncle Frate as a gift. In those days Brushy Creek was closer to the Wild Horse Wilderness of the old maps than to the fenced, farmed country it would all too soon become. The stud was turned out to range free with the mares, as was the custom of the time. He was young when he was turned out, but he lived a long and active life. Among his numerous offspring of some note in the country, probably the best was Dade.

Uncle Emzy spotted Dade as a three-year-old. A kid named Dade Hill was riding him, bareback, to school. It's pretty good evidence of what kind of horseman Uncle Emzy was that he saw what kind of horse Dade was. Old Man Henry Howell, a horse and mule trader in Fort Worth, told Daddy that Dade was the ugliest horse he'd ever seen, except maybe for some headed for the canner. He said Dade was too small to make a good roping horse, maybe seven hundred and fifty or eight hundred pounds and a bit too long-coupled for the length of his leg. His head wasn't well-shaped and his neck was a bit scrawny. But Uncle Emzy saw something in Dade's temperament and quickness that he liked, so he bought him and turned him into a roping horse. How good a roping horse he became is probably best told as Old Man Henry Howell told it to Daddy:

"We'as all at a big roping in San Antonio back around the turn of the century. Back in those days rodeoing wasn't quite as formal as it is now. They were roping in the infield of a racetrack, with no pens or chutes to hold and work stock. The folks working the show held a pretty good-sized bunch of steers at one end of the infield. The top dog of the crew would cut out each steer in turn and get it running down the infield. When the steer crossed the marker line and the roper fell in behind it, the timer started. [The roping wasn't any different; after the cowboy roped it, he dropped his slack along the steer's flank and behind its hind legs as he passed it by. When the slack came out of the rope, the steer had its hind legs cut out from under it and it swapped ends pretty quickly. The roper then jumped off his horse and tied the steer's legs before it could get up.] When the timer stopped the watch, the steer was let up and chased on down to the far end of the infield.

"I don't know what had happened to Emzy, but after we got there he'd gotten his leg bunged up and was gimping around on crutches and couldn't rope. Old John Blocker was there with a kid who was working for him. The kid was supposed to be a crackerjack roper, but his horse had come up lame and he needed to find a good horse if he was going to have a chance of finishing in the money. John had known Emzy forever and had heard that he had a good horse, so he went to talk to Emzy about borrowing Dade. Of course, when he and the kid saw the horse, they didn't figure Dade was the kind of horse that could do the kid any good. They told Emzy thanks but no thanks and went looking for another horse.

"The first roper that afternoon was another fellow from Taylor, and Emzy was letting him use Dade. After John saw what Dade could do, he came back to talk to Emzy. Of course, Emzy let the kid use Dade. Blocker's kid was the fifth roper that afternoon, and old Dade put him on that steer so quick he almost missed it. I guess the kid wished he had missed, 'cause what no one had noticed was that, about the time he took out after that steer, something had spooked those four steers that had already been roped.

"Now any cow brute will just naturally head for the bunch if it gets spooked, and that's what those four did. About the time the kid's rope comes tight, those four steers, running abreast, hit it about midway between the roped steer and old Dade. Well, a big old dust cloud come up and that kid sailed up above it and then did a kinda swan dive back down into it. Then we all got pretty quiet, waiting to see what it looked like when the dust settled. When it did, old Dade was the only one still on his feet. He'd been jerked completely around but was still up, and had his legs spread so much, waiting for the next shock, that you couldn't have run your hand between his belly and the ground. And he's looking, back and forth, at the five steers on the ground on his left and the cowboy, knocked colder than a wedge, on his right. For all the world, old Dade looked like he was looking back and forth trying to figure out what that blame fool had dropped a rope on.

"Course, Emzy always said that was the best thing that ever happened to old Dade. I asked him why, one time, and he told me that after that day Dade'd never let anyone but Emzy ride him."

Jack Davis worked on the theory that the first snowflake of the year that hit you was God's fault, but that the second one was your own fault. He followed the seasons, summering in Jackson Hole and the Absaroka range of northwestern Wyoming, and when fall arrived, which is pretty early in Jackson Hole, he'd head south. He didn't go alone. For twenty-eight years Jack packed for Wilson's Teton Valley Ranch, called the TV because of the brand. The ranch horses and mules weren't needed during the winter, so Jack took the whole outfit, better than a hundred head, with him as far as the Red Desert. He'd turn them loose, except for one of his pet bell mares, a few mules, and one or two saddle horses. He'd bid good-bye to the cowboys who'd helped with the drive and head south, horseback. Jack'd winter in Arizona or New Mexico, or even down in *old* Mexico—1936 was cold enough that he went all the way to Guatemala. In the spring he'd follow the grass north, arriving on the Red Desert in time to gather horses to drive back up to Jackson.

Jack never held a job he couldn't do horseback. When you spend your entire life with horses, you don't necessarily learn everything there is to know. Jack applied himself, though, and you never met anyone more knowledgeable of horses and, in particular in Jack's case, mules. No matter how many animals you work with, there are always a few special ones. Troubles was one of Jack's special mules. When Troubles got too old to work as a pack mule, she had the rare privilege of retirement, not a position many horses or mules attain in a world where animals have to pay their way or go to town.

Troubles didn't exactly go into full retirement, either. Her job was to teach an important lesson to horse and mule traders: never buy a gentle mule. Jack's theory was that you were better off spoiling your own so that you know what you can and can't do with them.

When the working horses and mules were brought in to the corrals every morning, Troubles came in with them and stood, all day, in a small, seldom-used pen behind the pack shed, waiting until she was needed. In the spring of the year, while an outfit is getting lined out and ready for the snow to get out of the high country so horses and mules can get in, ranches attract horse traders like barns attract flies. If a horse trader has a mule and sees mules in your corrals as he drives up, he climbs out of his rig saying, "Mister, have I got a gentle mule for you." If a trader said that to anyone on the TV, the man just pointed to Jack and said, "Go talk to him."

When the horse trader said that to Jack, he just called to Troubles. The gate on her pen was never shut, so she ambled up to Jack. He'd drape himself over her back and slide off headfirst on the other side. He'd then reach up and grab her ears—a piece of anatomy most mules consider their private property—and pull himself to his feet. He'd stand there and bat her ears around, blow in her nose, and finally get down on all fours and crawl between her forelegs, along under her belly, between her hind legs, and sit down, leaning back against her hocks. Jack would then take out his pipe, fill it, tamp it, get out a match, light up, and then sit there puffing. After a few puffs he'd look up at the horse trader and say, "Okay, mister. You do that with your gentle mule and I'll buy it." Jack told me he never did buy any gentle mules.

Since the subject of mules has come up, I should point out that the term *horseman*, back in the days before cars came along, applied not only to horseback riders, but to men who handled mules and draft stock, too. There were, back then, excellent horsemen, recognized by all for their ability, who had never ridden a horse in their lives. There were some who could do both; Uncle Emzy was one of them.

Ranching is an expensive occupation. It doesn't hurt to have another source of income to take up the slack. Uncle Emzy trained horses and mules to make a little extra cash when he needed it. If you haven't fooled with mules much, you probably believe all the claptrap about their being stupid and stubborn that's put out by people who either have never been around mules or aren't as smart as the mules they have been around. A mule is the hybrid offspring of a jack donkey and a horse mare. One of the places hybrid vigor shows up is in intelligence. For instance, if a horse is brought in hot and lathered up and turned loose in a corral with grain in the feed box and cold water in the water trough, it'll eat and drink too much too quickly, founder itself, and wind up crippled if not dead. No, with a horse, you have to turn it into a dry corral with no feed until it cools off. Turn a lathered-up mule loose in the same corral and it'll stand there and blow for a while, then roll. After that it might go over and wet its lips, take a sip or two of water, and then go stand in the shade and finish cooling off. When it's cooled enough that it won't hurt itself, it'll go over and get a drink and then go eat some of the grain, but not all. After a while it'll drink its fill and finish the grain. The next day it'll be healthy, happy, and ready to work again. By the same token, if you ask a mule to do something, it won't do it if it thinks it's going to get hurt. They think about everything, but they think about it from a mule's perspective. You're admitting that you think the mule is smarter than you if you think it's easier for him to see things from your point of view than for you to see his. You'd be surprised how many people are willing to admit that.

Another thing that causes many people to shy away from mules is that a mule will, at times, make a point of his argument with his hind feet. A training gig is a light two-wheeled cart, really just a set of wheels with a seat big enough for two over the axle. That places the driver's face at precisely the right height for a mule, harnessed directly in front of the driver, to make an indelible imprint on the driver if the two get into a serious debate. Because the prospect of such a debate doesn't appeal to most people, training gigs are built with very long shafts, so that the mule is harnessed so far forward that he can't reach the driver with his hind feet. The shafts are long enough that the mule is not clear out at the front of them. The points of the shafts stick out as far as the mule's head. I've even seen gigs with tassels hung on the ends of the shafts, the idea being to get the mule used to seeing a little movement out of the corners of his eyes. Then he won't panic and start a rodeo the first time you take him to town and a piece of paper blows across the street under his nose.

A mule has never paid any attention to a wagon before he starts his training, so it's no surprise that once he gets used to pulling a wagon, he gets a mite confused when the wagon starts pushing on him. But that's exactly what happens when he starts down a hill. No one has explained to the mule that he has become the brakes rather than the engine; the only way you can explain is by example. The mule's initial reaction is to think that the wagon is trying to run over him. Naturally he attempts to prevent this from happening. Unfortunately, the faster the mule runs, the faster the wagon chases. Mules, like most intelligent animals, are subject to panic. The technical term to describe what happens in this situation is *runaway*. Reins, I might add, are of absolutely no use in stopping a runaway mule. If you get out on flat ground with no fences, trees, gullies, or such, you might be able to get the mule to run in circles until it gives out, but you can't stop it with the reins.

To train a mule not to run away on downhill grades, Uncle Emzy used a pickup. It's a simple device: a hobble cuff goes around one of the mule's ankles, and a rope coming off it runs up through a ring on the harness and back to the driver. When you start downhill and the training gig begins to push on the mule, it starts to run. Uncle Emzy would then pull back on the reins and say "Whoa!" which had no effect on the mule. Uncle Emzy would then count to three and pull on the pickup rope, which would pick up the mule's front foot. A mule is smart enough to know he can't run on three legs, so he stops. After Uncle Emzy had done this a few times, the mule registered that he had three seconds to stop on four legs after Uncle Emzy said "whoa." Then Uncle Emzy would put the hobble cuff on without the rope, but since the mule recognized the act of putting the cuff on, he'd stop when Uncle Emzy said "whoa." Finally the cuff wasn't required; the mule had figured out that the gig wasn't going to run over him, and he was trained about going down hills. The catch was that the country around home was flat. Mules were pretty far along in the rest of their training before they encountered enough hills to learn that part.

One summer Uncle Emzy took on thirty or thirty-five mules to break and train for harness work. With that many mules to work with, he hired a couple of high school kids to help him. Uncle Emzy was a good employer. He gave the two kids Saturday afternoons and Sunday mornings off, just about every week. About midway through the summer they asked Uncle Emzy if they could borrow the gig and one of the mules so that they could go into town on Saturday afternoon. Uncle Emzy pointed out a little mule to them that was ready for a trip into town. (Notice that there is a vast difference between the phrases "a trip *to* town" and "a trip *into* town"; the latter refers to a round trip.) "Now y'all be careful. When you start down Brown's Hill, that little mule is going to break to run. Whatever you do, don't let her run away with you."

The old saying about two heads being better than one is only true if at least one of the heads is engaged in thinking. That is, all too often, not the case with teenaged boys. These two put their heads together and figured that if one was good, two was better. They put a "running W" on the mule, and that picks up both front feet.

By the time they got to Brown's Hill, those two kids were ready. They started down it and the mule broke to run. One kid pulled back on the reins and said "whoa!"; the other one counted, very slowly, to three and pulled up on the lines of the running W. By then the mule was flying, but when the kid pulled up on the lines, she not only stopped but buried her nose in the road, which also buried the points of the shafts of the gig in the road and converted it from a very small wagon into a pretty good-sized catapult. When the dust had settled, the mule was on her back, head uphill, the gig was upside down on the downhill side of her, and the kids were on the Cottonwood bridge, down at the foot of the hill. Uncle Emzy told Daddy, "Oh, they weren't hurt any. Well, one did have a broken arm and I'll admit you couldn't lay a fifty-cent piece down on either one of them and not hit a spot that wasn't either bruised or skinned up, but they weren't really hurt any."

"You know," Uncle Emzy said, "if it wasn't so hard on equipment, that'd be a great way to train mules." When Daddy asked for an explanation, Uncle Emzy replied, "Why, after that, that ol' mule could be out in the pasture, a half-mile from you and running flat out, but if you could yell loud enough for her to hear you, she'd stop when you said 'whoa.'"

During the years I worked for the Turners' Triangle X Ranch, I spent as much time as possible in the backcountry, with pack trips in the summer and hunting camp in the fall. The backcountry we worked in was wilderness. It was often seventy-five or eighty miles to a fence, and we turned our horses loose every night to scatter and find grass, except for one or two wrangle horses. In the mornings you had to climb aboard the wrangle horses, go find all the stock, and bring it back to camp. That kind of wrangling and the work you do when you catch the horses leaves memories, of both the good and bad variety. We had a horse called Plum, named that because of his color, but earned because he was a plumb good horse.

One of the wrangler's jobs at hunting camp was to help get the game back to camp. Once an elk or moose was shot, the guide would clean and quarter it, cover the quarters with brush to keep the ravens and coyotes off, and maybe hang the antlers if a tree was handy. The next day someone would go back for the game. That freed the hunters from having to take pack animals with them while they were hunting and made packing much easier; elk quarters are less like a hundred-pound bag of half-chilled Jell-O the next day. If the wranglers weren't otherwise occupied, they'd pack the game back for the guides.

It was a beautiful fall morning in the mountains. I was caught up on all my other work, so I was going out to pack in an elk that one of John's hunters had shot the day before. One of Harold's two hunters had scored the day before too, so I offered to pack that one in as well, so that they could hunt all day. It was the sort of day that makes October in the mountains so special. It was fifty degrees by nine in the morning. The snow of the week before was pretty well melted out of the meadows, while it was still a foot or so deep back in the timber. Color was still hanging on a bit in sheltered places, and the sky was the clear blue of mountain fall. I was riding Plum and we were moving slowly, as you tend to do when you're leading four mules, just enjoying the day, figuring to make it back to camp by midafternoon. It was worth a day's wages just to be out on a day like that, though I didn't plan on telling Harold that. In spite of the nice weather, I was carrying my winter clothes—coat, sweater, and mittens—in a roll on the back of my saddle; it pays to be careful in the mountains. By the time I reached the first elk, it had clouded up and the temperature was dropping fast.

Shot through the heart, the elk had run a hundred yards back into the timber before it died. There were plenty of trees to tie the mules to, and I needed them tied; all four were new to packing meat. Mules don't like the smell of blood when they first encounter it. They don't like to have bloody elk quarters tied onto their sides. If you take the time to rub a good deal of blood on and around their noses the first time they pack meat, you find that by the time the smell wears off, they're over their fear of the smell of blood. Once I got these four tied up and their noses treated, it was beginning to snow. By the time I had the elk packed on two of them and was ready to go, my gloves were soaked from working in the snow and blood. I pulled them off, stuck them in the saddlebags, and put on my mittens along with my coat and sweater.

Within a few minutes the snow progressed from flurries to a hard, steady fall pushed by an increasing wind. By the time I got to Upper Fox Park, I was glad Harold had given me good directions, because the only sign of his elk was a snowdrift with some elk antlers hung in the trees, fifty yards off. Working in the open, I had to tie three mules in the trees and take out one at a time to pack. I cinched up my saddle and snubbed the mule I was working with to Plum, who held it more or less still. It had gotten colder than I thought, and my gloves were frozen into balls in my saddlebags. I tried to work barehanded but lost the feeling in my fingers too quickly, so I had to wear my mittens to pack. I got the mules packed and hitched, but by then my mittens were soaked. By the time I had mounted, gotten the mules lined out behind me, and started for home, the weather had deteriorated into a sure 'nough blizzard. Visibility was down to about fifty feet and getting worse. I gave Plum his head and concentrated on making sure the mules were okay and that my hands didn't freeze any worse than necessary. Normally, in cold weather you can take a single dally with the lead rope and then stick the end under your leg. There's enough tension to get the mules to follow, but in a real bind it'll pull free, usually not before you have a chance to grab the rope. I was nervous about those young mules, though, afraid of any kind of a wreck in that blizzard that would require my having to try to repack one of them. I wanted to keep the lead rope in hand so I could get the first inkling of any problems. I kept shifting hands, keeping one under my coat, trying to warm it up before the other one went numb.

Within an hour the wind and snow were enough that I felt like I was riding inside a Ping-Pong ball. I was beginning to give some serious thought to my hands, wondering if I couldn't trust the mules and get my hands inside my coat to warm them up, when Plum just stopped and refused to take another step. I was preparing to get off and to see if I could figure out what was wrong, when Ric stuck his head out of a tent about ten or fifteen feet off on my left and asked if I needed some help. White tents don't show up well in a blizzard. Plum had brought us home.

Ric and Phil came out and took the mules over to

the meat rack while I took Plum over to my tent to put my saddle in where it was warm and to get my spare mittens. Then I took Plum over to the wrangle tent and tied him so he could cool off inside, out of the storm. When we'd finished hanging the meat and getting the mules tended to, I went back to the wrangle tent and made sure Plum got a little extra bait of grain before I headed to the cook tent to thaw out and to see how much coffee Phil had made.

Like most ranches, the Triangle X couldn't afford to keep extra horses. If a horse couldn't pull its weight, it had to go to town. Even the best horses get to that point, just too old to do the job anymore. You don't like to think about it, but there is no alternative. Except occasionally.

The year the movie *Spencer's Mountain* was filmed on and around the ranch, Clay was born and named for Henry Fonda's character. He lived a long life, the last two years of which he was too old and too stiff to work. He stayed in the corral those two winters and was fed grain. He had paid for the grain on a snowy fall day some years before. John Turner was riding Clay, guiding a single elk hunter that day, when they rode up on a grizzly bear's food cache. Fresh powder snow had fallen a foot deep and covered the bear's tracks and the gut pile it was protecting. The pile was out in a little meadow, the bear lying in the timber sixty or seventy yards from it. John and his hunter rode into the meadow on the opposite side and had come thirty or forty yards into the clearing before the bear reacted.

The bear came down the hill as only a grizzly can, spraying powder snow like it was running through shallow water. The bear was probably no more than three hundred and fifty pounds, but John said that, coming down the hill, it looked as big as Clay. Grizzlies are like that. The hunter was trying to get his rifle out of the scabbard when the horse he was riding remembered something they had left in camp and went back to get it. The problem was that he left considerably faster than the hunter did. When the hunter picked himself up from the snow, he still had his rifle, which he had poked barrel-first into the snow. John told me that he'd realized that if the hunter tried to shoot, his rifle would probably explode because the barrel was packed full of snow.

Generally, hunting stories end at this point as the brave guide saves his hunter's life by dropping the charging bear in its tracks with a carefully placed shot. Fortunately, John is a wildlife biologist who grew up just down the road from Olas and Marty Murie and the Craighead brothers. He knew enough about grizzlies to know that most of their charges are bluffs to see what you'll do. John told his hunter not to shoot, and waited. John told me Clay stood as still as if he'd been carved of stone. The bear made a stiff-legged stop in a spray of snow about twenty feet from them. John kept talking low, telling the hunter not to shoot and the bear that everything was okay. The bear turned and walked away, only to wheel and charge again. Again it skidded to a halt about twenty feet from them. This process was repeated several times, moving the bear in a half-circle around them. There were some young pines getting started in the meadow, and the bear was beginning to get the trees between it and them. Clay moved then, for the first time. Without John saying anything, he slowly moved to keep John positioned so that he always had a shot at the bear.

After several of the bluff charges, the bear returned to its daybed and John told the hunter to walk, not run, along the path his horse had taken. John waited for the hunter to get back into the timber a ways before he followed. When he tried to pull Clay around, he wouldn't turn. The horse backed all the way to the timber, so that John could keep an eye on the bear. When they reached the timber, Clay finally turned and they went after the hunter and his horse. Three or four hundred yards later they caught up with them. The hunter's horse had stopped there, and the hunter had gotten a cleaning rod from his saddlebags and reopened the bore of his rifle. He was sitting on a stump, looking a little the worse for wear. John said he felt the need to get off, but when he did, his knees weren't really all that steady, so he held on to the saddle horn to brace himself. He said he was amazed that he was shaking as hard as he was. Then he realized that he wasn't shaking at all, Clay was. When he finally did stop shaking, Clay looked around at John and his eyes very clearly said, "Don't EVER do that again!"

* * *

Often you don't know what a horse or a person is capable of until something happens that draws it out. Horsemen love horses, and the ones that surprise you are, if not the best, often the most interesting.

I came onto the following story in bits and pieces while working down in the Red Desert. I've had to piece it together, figure it out, and, in places, even suppose a bit. But the horse in it is one of a kind.

There are two types of sheepherders. Those who herd because they are good at it—who love the sheep, the dogs, and the country—are the ones ranchers love to have work for them. There aren't enough of those sheepherders, though, so ranchers sometimes have to hire the other type of herders, the ones who can't hold any other job. Most of them don't know sic-'em about sheep, dogs, or much of anything else, and more than a few of them will take a drink every now and then. (I've never understood whether a lot of sheepherders become alcoholics or if a lot of alcoholics become sheepherders, and I'm not sure it's really relative to the discussion at hand, because this is really about horses.) When ranchers have to hire the second type of herder, they need good dogs. Basically, the dogs do all the work and the herder is there to feed the dogs and move the wagon. The herder in this story is one of the second type.

Very few sheepherders are horsemen. The types of horses that cowboys love, sheepherders view as grounds for quitting. By and large, sheepherders ride older or broken-down horses, ones that are past using on a cattle outfit. The primary requirement is that a horse be gentle and not likely to cause any trouble. The horse in question here had probably never been anything to write home about, but his prime was long before our story. He'd been able to vote for Roosevelt two or three times. He was old and played out, an ideal horse for a sheepherder. He had been assigned to one of the sheepherders of the second type. They had a band of sheep out in the Red Desert.

The Red Desert, to most untrained observers, appears to be mile after mile of nothing but mile after mile. It's not bad sheep country, though, as long as you don't let them stay in one place too long. The dogs kept the sheep moving, and the sheepherder moved camp to keep up with them. After enough moves, the sheepherder found that he was camped not too far from a little crossroads saloon. It had been a long dry spell for the sheepherder, and the proximity of the saloon increased his thirst until he decided that the dogs could take care of the sheep without him for a while. He planned on just being gone for a little while, having a drink or two, and talking to some humans for a change. So, as soon as he'd eaten his dinner, he saddled up and headed for the saloon, figuring he'd be back for a late supper. There was an obstacle, in the form of a pretty good-sized canyon, between him and the saloon. The only way across it, without a day-long detour, was over a railroad bridge. If you've never walked railroad bridges, you might not know how much concentration is required.

They don't put a bed on a railroad bridge; it's just the crossties, with a hole about a foot or a foot and a half between each tie. It's hard walking for a human; it's damn near impossible for a horse. Very few people would dare to try to get a horse across a railroad bridge. A few good horsemen might, with a sure-'nough good horse, try it in a dire emergency. Very few people are as thirsty as that sheepherder was. He figured it was a dire emergency. He tried it. The old horse made it about a third of the way across when he misstepped and put all four legs through. He's stuck, lying on his belly, unable to move at all. The sheepherder pulled off the saddle and bridle and took them along as he walked on toward the saloon. In his defense, maybe he figured he could get some help there. Unfortunately, a train came before he got there.

I don't know if you remember steam locomotives, but for the Rocky Mountain West they built some big engines. The Union Pacific had a type of engine used in this part of the world back then that they called a Long Tom. It was the biggest steam locomotive ever made. Its firebox was twenty-one feet long, and its boiler was so big it was hinged in the middle so it could get around the curves. It had more drivers than most engines had wheels. A Long Tom going fifty miles an hour, with a hundred boxcars on behind, took a mile or more to get stopped. And that's what was headed toward the horse.

The engineer was about a quarter of a mile from the horse when he saw it. He commenced to apply the brakes, but he knew it wasn't going to do any good, that he wasn't going to be much more than slowed slightly by the time he got to the horse. And the horse would probably derail the train, which meant that he was going to arrive at the bottom of the canyon, where the huge boiler would explode and blow him back up into one hundred rapidly descending boxcars.

At about this time the horse looked back and saw the train. If you've never looked up and seen that much steel coming at you at fifty miles an hour, you might not fully appreciate the horse's reaction, but I suspect you would have a similar one. He released about as much adrenaline at that instant as he had in his whole life previous to that moment. I've enough anatomy studies behind me to know, beyond the shadow of a doubt, that a horse stuck as that one was had absolutely no hope of ever getting out without the assistance of some machinery. That old horse didn't have the benefit of my education. But he did have a train bearing down on him. He got up. Of course, he was still out on the bridge and there was plenty of it between him and hard ground. And he'd already fallen through once.

The stride of a horse is measured from where one foot strikes the ground to where that foot strikes the ground again. Secretariat's stride was something over thirty feet when he was running. Now, that old horse's stride would never match Secretariat's, but his speed, for the next few furlongs, might have. But, to be positive that he didn't fall again, he was making sure he hit every tie. His stride was only about two feet, but, by God, he was taking those strides in a hurry. The engineer continued to apply the brakes. He was decelerating, but the old horse was accelerating so that, by the time they reached the end of the bridge, the horse had a good head of steam up and was apparently beginning to enjoy adrenaline. He was outrunning a locomotive and feeling better than he ever had in his life. Pride was suddenly flowing through his system along with the adrenaline, and he didn't just step aside when they cleared the bridge. He had good footing now and could lengthen his stride. When they went past the sheepherder, the horse was starting to pull away. When he finally tired of the game and stepped off the tracks, he was a wild horse and looking for a mustang band to join.

The sheepherder just set the saddle down when he saw the horse outrunning the train. He left it and walked on to the saloon. He got a quick drink and then borrowed the phone and called his boss. When he told the rancher he was quitting, the rancher asked him why.

"You can't expect me to ride the kind of horses you're sending out here."

Uncle Emzy said one time that anyone could count himself lucky if he'd had one good horse in his life. I consider myself blessed because I've been associated not just with a few good horses, but with quite a few good horsemen, too.

THIS
OL' DROUGHT...

.\/\.\/\.\/\.\/\.\

One thing I've noticed about ranchers is their tendency to laugh at things that aren't funny. I think it's the nature of their work. When you look at how many things can go wrong, and how few have much chance of going right, you understand why ranchers develop a sense of humor designed for protection. Daddy told me that no one without a sense of humor should be a farmer or rancher. As he put it, "If you don't have a sense of humor, you shouldn't go into a business where you buy everything retail, sell everything wholesale, and let the other guy set the prices." That more or less sums up the way ranchers look at things. If you can laugh at the things that you have no control of, you have some protection.

Droughts define ranch country as well as any-thing. What we consider a wet year would be called a drought back East. But we think of droughts as the norm. They are so much a part of life that if a rancher can't laugh at them, he's in serious trouble. There are, of course, other things that ranchers have had to learn to laugh about. In my travels, visiting with people, listening and watching, I've noticed that there are three things all ranchers laugh at: the weather—droughts, floods, blizzards, tornadoes, and the like; the bank—that wonderful institution in part-nership with virtually every rancher; and the gov-ernment—what can I, or anyone else, say? Well, maybe there is a story that would.

The tone for the relationship between the federal government and ranchers was set, I figure, during the administration of Chester A. Arthur.

I ran into the following story while working around the town of Never Sweat, Wyoming. Folks still tell it there with some pride. Actually, the town isn't called Never Sweat anymore. But the first post-mistress asked for that name when she applied to have a post office established there. She said she'd never seen a man break sweat there—there's no record of whether she saw that as a positive or a negative part of the local men's character—so it seemed like a good, descriptive name for the place. For some reason the U.S. Postal Service didn't agree with her—we won't get into the issue of all the big-wigs at the Postal Service being men in those days; there are going to be enough digressions in this story without that. For whatever reason, the powers that be wouldn't let a town be named Never Sweat, but instead chose a name for the new town, Dubois. Coincidentally, the head of the postal committee in Congress at that time was named Dubois. I'm sure there's no connection there, although the towns of Dubois, Nebraska, and Dubois, Idaho, were named at about the same time. But back to the story:

One summer, President Arthur decided he wanted to see the wonders of Yellowstone National Park. Presidents do seem to like Yellowstone, which is natural since best evidence indicates that most of our presidents have been more or less human. Nowadays, though, it's not a big deal for a president to go to Yellowstone; he can fly to Billings or Bozeman, Montana, in Air Force One. From there it's a quick hop in a helicopter over to the Park.

In Chester A. Arthur's day, a trip to Yellowstone was a bit more trouble. He and his entourage came as far as Green River, Wyoming, on the Union Pacific. Wagons were waiting for them there to take them on the next leg, through South Pass, over the mountains past the mining camps at South Pass City and Atlantic City, down through Lander and on to Fort Washakie, the agency for the Wind River Indian Reservation, to pick up their Indian guides (no one of consequence could travel in the West back then without Indian guides, it just wasn't done).

About forty or fifty soldiers were sent along from the fort to protect the President from the Indians, even though the guides were Shoshone, allies of the whites since the days of Lewis and Clark. The

Shoshone were traveling light, as they were prone to do; the soldiers weren't. They added quite a few head of stock to a party that wasn't small to start with. If you've ever seen a picture of Chester A. Arthur, you know he was not into roughing it. Sleeping on the hard, cold ground was not the sort of thing he saw as adding noticeably to the dignity of his office, either. I've seen circuses with fewer and smaller tents than he had. A sleeping tent with brass bed, chest of drawers, rugs, etc., and a separate bathing tent. That took wagons, and horses to pull them. He also preferred to eat not only on a regular basis but on a frequent one as well. He was also known to take an occasional nip. So there were more wagons to haul the kitchen, the groceries, the "wine cellar" and bar, and a dining tent big enough to hold all the important people. And there were plenty of important people.

Back then, just like today, presidents didn't go many places by themselves. Chester A. Arthur had a photographer along, and the pictures are in the Library of Congress. Looking through them is like looking at a *Who's Who* of official Washington. There were cabinet members, senators, congressmen, ambassadors, important and seemingly important hangers-on. As a matter of fact, the only person of note not in the pictures was the vice-president.

Looking at those pictures, I suddenly realized something that no civics teacher had ever been able to explain to me: why we have a vice-president. It had always seemed to me that we paid a good deal of money to someone to just sit around and wait for someone else to die. And that is, apparently, the vice-president's job. Oh, sure, they try to justify it by saying he's in charge of the Senate, but I think we can all agree that no one's in charge of the Senate. Looking at those pictures, though, I realized that when the job was created, there was a need for it.

Everyone who was anyone was in Yellowstone that summer. Everyone who was anyone was somewhere other than Washington, D.C., every summer. Before air conditioning, people wouldn't spend the summer in Washington on a bet. The vice-president's job was like a night watchman's job, but for the whole summer. To get the job you just had to agree to stay in Washington all summer and make sure the doors were locked on the important buildings—the Capitol, the Treasury, places like that. It was safe to leave him there alone, since no one could start a war with the United States during the summer because they couldn't get an ambassador to go to Washington to tell us about it until the fall. (Remember, this was back in the civilized era when countries declared war on their enemies before they started them.)

Now that we have air conditioning and instant communications, we could probably do away with the vice-presidency and save the money. But that wouldn't accomplish much. We'd surely spend it on something equally as foolish; after all, the government would still have it. And there would also be the problem of another person on unemployment, since someone qualified to be vice-president probably couldn't hold a real job.

All of this about the vice-president has nothing to

do with the story, he wasn't even there. But I promised some digressions a few paragraphs back, and felt obliged to deliver. Back to the story.

When that many important people went traipsing off into the wilderness, someone had to protect them (the soldiers from Fort Washakie were just supposed to protect them from the guides, who were friendly). So the President had invited Phil Sheridan and a few dozen of his men along. Sheridan was General of the Army then, a position he considered at least as important as Arthur's. That meant that anything the President had, Sheridan had to have too. And both of them, and I suspect everyone else of rank, which was just about everyone else, judging from the pictures, needed soldiers, packers, teamsters, farriers, cooks, dishwashers, woodcutters, and various handymen and servants to do the work. What I'm driving at is that, by the time this outfit passed Fort Washakie, they had a pretty sizable horse herd. There were horses to pull wagons and carriages. There were horses to ride. There were horses to pack if they went places wagons couldn't go. There were spare horses, in case some played out.

The caravan headed up Wind River, looking for a place to camp and rest the horses a few days before they started over the mountains to the Yellowstone country via a pass one of the Shoshone guides, a man named Togwotee, had shown one of the army officers on a surveying trip a few years before. (One last digression: the road from Dubois to Jackson Hole follows that trail today, and is still called Togwotee Pass.) When they got to Horse Creek, where Never Sweat would be started in just a few more years, the group turned up the creek and shortly came to just what they were looking for. Horse Creek cuts a beautiful, narrow valley, a quarter-mile to a half-mile wide and several miles long, covered, in those days, with native grasses growing stirrup high. The tourists looked on it and saw a perfect place to camp for a few days. They could hunt and fish while the horses rested and fattened on the grass before starting on the hard pull over the mountains to Yellowstone National Park. What none of them had noticed was that, tucked away in the timber on the hillside above the valley, there was a cabin belonging to a man named Helms. The lush meadows the presidential party was casting covetous eyes on belonged to him as well.

The President and his people may not have seen Mr. Helms, but he saw them. Mostly what he saw was a horde descending on his winter feed. Mr. Helms did what any self-respecting rancher would do in a situation like that. He reached up over his door, took down his Winchester, jumped on his horse, and went to talk to them about it.

Some things never change. Back then, just like today, when someone started toward the President with a Winchester, it just naturally made folks nervous. Phil Sheridan and a goodly number of his cavalry troops rode out to head Helms off and have a little visit with him before he got too close to President Arthur. Sheridan, when he finally got Helms stopped, said to him, "My God, man, this is the President of these United States who wants to camp here." Mr. Helms's reply, I believe, set the tone for the relationship between ranchers and the federal government for all time. He looked Sheridan in the eye and said, "I don't give a good blankety-blank what he's president of, get him out of my hay meadows."

If you know the country around Dubois and take time to stop at the Library of Congress and look at the pictures from Chester A. Arthur's trip to Yellowstone National Park, you'll notice that the presidential party camped about five or six miles below the mouth of Horse Creek.

Ranchers like this story. It's always nice to hear about winning, even if it was long ago and you've been paying for it ever since, as some insist is the case.

Exploring the stories of the late nineteenth and early twentieth centuries, looking for the character-istic sense of humor applied to those things that ranchers normally can't control, I found quite a few tales of an interesting group of entrepreneurs. They operated a banking syndicate out of an area just west of where Kaycee, Wyoming, is now, an area called the Hole-in-the-Wall. The head of this syndi-cate was a man known as Butch Cassidy, and although he was not the originator of the philosophy, he is generally given credit for the style and success of the syndicate. The group made large cash with-drawals from banks where none of them had an account.

Though I've had many sources for stories of the

Hole-in-the-Wall Gang, Boyd Charter was one of the best. I met Boyd while he was on the board of the Northern Plains Resource Council, trying to keep his and his neighbors' places from being strip-mined. But he was from Jackson Hole, where I'd spent several years, and we spent some time talking, first about old-timers we'd both known, then about old times in general.

Boyd came from Jackson Hole to the Bull Mountains because of...no, those are other stories for another time. Boyd had grown up in Jackson Hole on a ranch his daddy started with some money he had stashed away sometime before he left Wyoming for the Klondike Gold Rush, not so much to strike it rich as to live for a while in a place where no one asked your name or where you were from. Butch and the Sundance Kid left for South America at about the same time. This is all a way of saying that Bert, Boyd's daddy, had some background for the stories he told Boyd and that Boyd told me. I wouldn't go so far as to say that Bert was ever part of that particular banking syndicate, but Boyd did have a photo of a group of men, taken in front of the old hotel in Rawlins, Wyoming, that included Bert and all the recognizable members of the Hole-in-the-Wall Gang. For whatever reason, Bert knew quite a few of the members of the group, and some of them came to visit him in later days, when all were retired, or dead, and leading quiet lives.

Robbing banks in places like Wyoming or Montana was easy and safe. The only people who would chase you were those who were paid to do so, and most of them were smart enough to realize that heavily armed men are best chased at a respectful distance until your horses played out and you could go home, shrug your shoulders about not being able to catch the bad guys because they had better horses, and draw your pay. Still, it just wasn't a sensible business practice to be wanted in the state you were living in. It added unnecessary complications to your life and to the lives of peace officers you liked and got along with reasonably well. There was also the fact that robbing banks in places like Wyoming or Montana didn't make particularly good economic sense; the banks didn't have any money in them. Everyone owed his bank money and couldn't be sure, in those freewheeling days before federal regulations, that the banker might mistake a deposit in your checking account for a payment on your loan. Generally, if folks got any cash, they kept it at home.

To make money robbing banks, a gang had to find banks with money in them. That usually meant either finding a boomtown, a town with a mining or railroad payroll, or going to Utah. Utah was a special case because of the Mormon Church. Since, back in those days, pretty much everyone in a town in Utah would belong to the same church, people actually trusted their banker and kept their money in the bank. That made robbing banks in Utah profitable. The drawback to robbing banks in Utah was that there was no such thing as the FDIC back then, either. That meant the only way for people to get back the money they lost when the bank was robbed was to go get it. Which meant that if you robbed a bank, everyone in the county came looking for you with blood in his eyes.

The secret to being a successful bank robber was good horses, and not just on the day you robbed the bank. You needed good, fresh horses every day after that, too. So the Hole-in-the-Wall Gang would leave home with a pretty good-sized cavvy when they headed down the country to tend to some of their banking business. Every day they would leave a relay of horses so that, on their return, they could have fresh horses every day. That way, no matter how well mounted the pursuit was at first, over the course of a few days their horses would play out, but the gang, getting fresh horses each day, would continue to put distance between themselves and the chasers. And given time to work at it, tracks can be made to dis-appear or lead in the wrong direction.

Now, you can't tie a horse to a tree and come back two weeks later expecting to ride it. Someone had to take care of the horses. Deep in "hostile" territory a gang member would wait, day-herding a relay in a quiet place and picketing them at night for the few days necessary. But back up the country there were plenty of little hardscrabble homestead ranchers who would gladly hold horses for the gang. Most of them were probably sympathetic to the idea of steal-ing from bankers, but even if they weren't, everyone liked Butch and would hold horses for him and not bother to ask why. When the gang stopped by on their way to conduct their banking business, they'd leave the horses with instructions to have them up, in the corral, on such and such a day. On the gang's return, the ranchers got to keep the horses the gang left with them and maybe a little pay for their trouble. If some folks, riding tired horses, showed up in a few days, asking questions about a group of armed men, the ranchers would most likely prove to have pretty vague memories.

On one occasion, as Boyd told me, the gang had been down in Utah and was heading home. He wouldn't tell me exactly where this happened because, he said, the descendants of the family involved were still on the place and he didn't know if they wanted this told on their grandparents or not. I figure it was somewhere around the southern end of the Bighorns, but that's only a guess. The gang had probably outdistanced any pursuit by then, but they had ridden through the night to be sure. They arrived at this particular little ranch in the morning, and the horses were up, in the corral, waiting for them. While they were catching fresh mounts, the rancher came out to visit.

"Boys," he said, "it's a good thing y'all got here today and not tomorrow. By this time tomorrow we'll be gone. The banker's due out here this afternoon. We owe him three thousand dollars and can't begin to pay it. He's gonna take the place. My wife's in the house packing now. Just as soon as we settle accounts with him, we're leaving." He went back to the house and the gang talked it over among themselves while they saddled up. Before they left, they rode over to the house and called the rancher and his wife out onto the porch. Butch explained that they liked the couple and felt that if they had a break or two they'd make a go of the place, and besides all that, there wasn't anyone else around that the gang trusted to hold horses for them. With that he pulled the three thousand out of his saddlebags (they had a little cash surplus at the time) and gave it to them.

"Pay the banker when he comes," Butch said, "but remember who you're doing business with. You're paying cash and there are no witnesses. Make sure you get a written receipt from him so you can prove you paid him." The startled couple thanked them and offered to repay the money, but Butch assured them that their help was repayment enough. The gang rode away and the couple started to unpack.

When the banker showed up that afternoon, expecting to foreclose on the place, he was surprised to find the couple waiting for him, money in hand. But business was business. He took the money, gave them a receipt, and headed back to town. Four or five miles down the road he had to ford a creek. Stopping to let his horse drink, the banker sat in his buggy admiring the scenery when, to his consternation, a group of armed men rode out of the brush along the stream and held him up. He said later that it was almost as though they knew he was carrying money. I figure they probably knew the serial numbers on the bills.

I pass this story along for a couple of reasons. First, it's a good story. But second, and more important—if anything is more important than a good story—is the story's significance to an active debate of today. Congress, in its never-ending search for ways to cut the budget without hurting the people of any important congressman's district, keeps coming back to chopping ag programs as ways to save. The argument is that farmers and ranchers are going to go broke anyhow, so giving them money to try to stay afloat is just prolonging the inevitable. This story proves otherwise. Boyd told me that the descendants of the ranch couple were still on the place. They made it. So I figure what the Hole-in-the-Wall Gang did was to make the first low-interest ag loan in Wyoming. And it worked. Most people would say that Congress and the Hole-in-the-Wall Gang have quite a bit in common. Maybe Congress can make it work too.

Some things just don't change in ways we can see. No matter how the world changes politically, socially, and culturally, the climate, from our limited perspective, never changes. Ice ages come and go too slowly for our immediate notice. Droughts and floods, hurricanes and tornadoes, blizzards and chinooks are the weather patterns we can see and feel. If you work the land, all you can be sure of is that seven times out of ten the weather will do something other than what you want it to.

The weather does produce stories better than crops, and most of the good ones are not about ideal, wet springs, or mild, easy winters. Those you cherish, but don't talk about. Talking about them might ruin them, like handling silver too much tarnishes it. The good stories are about coping with bad weather, because that's something you need to be able to do. And laughing at it makes it less frightening.

We had a little spring storm on Powder River in '84. It started raining about midnight on the twenty-fifth of April. By midmorning it had turned to snow. By noon it was a blizzard. It snowed hard for three days. Depending on how far out from the mountains you were, you got anywhere from three to about six feet of snow. That didn't matter, though, because the wind blew so much that it drifted—oh Lord, how it drifted. Stock heads for the canyons and draws to get out of the weather here, but that storm filled the canyons brimful, burying anything unfortunate enough to have gone there for refuge. Johnson County, the only place I've actually seen the numbers for, lost about ninety-three percent of its sheep. Most of them suffocated. Cattle didn't fare much better.

But by then it was May. In a week the snow had melted and spring arrived. It greened up and folks in town forgot all about it except for the stories they had about where they were stuck from Wednesday till Sunday or Monday, when they could get home again.

The Busy Bee Diner in Buffalo, Wyoming, is one of the best places I know to collect stories. Back then, Hollis and Helen Voiles still owned it (they've since retired, but sold it to the folks who worked there, so it's retained its flavor—in food and atmosphere) and would rearrange the seating along the counter to allow me to sit next to someone who had good stories.

A place like the Bee is of real importance to a small town that only has a weekly newspaper (the radio station just can't cover all the local news between 6:00 A.M. and dark). Everyone stops by to share what's happening with everyone else. When folks come into town they at least stop by for coffee and a visit before heading home. If you need to know anything, from what the fire siren was about last night to the current price of dry cows, the Bee is the place to go in Buffalo.

I was sitting there one beautiful afternoon in the fall of '84, enjoying my coffee, when an old bachelor rancher from south of town came in and sat down next to me. I asked him how things were going.

"Let me tell you," he said, "I can't remember when I've had a summer this good. I had rain just when I needed it, in just the amounts I needed. I've got grass growing belly-high to a tall horse all over my place. And I had good irrigation water too. Now I've only been on that place sixty-seven years, but this is the best hay crop I can remember on it." He took a sip of his coffee, thought for a moment, and added, "Of course, after that storm last spring, there's not a hoof left on the place to eat any of it."

I liked the line and the attitude it illustrated, so I told the story to a few people that winter, thinking it was a pretty good one. I didn't realize I'd only heard the first half. Every once in a while, if you work hard enough at your art, the Muses give you one for free. The second half of this story was such a gift.

The next spring I finished up some work a day or two early in Cheyenne and was headed home at a leisurely pace, enjoying seeing the world just beginning to green up. It's a really special time of the year, the season of mud; chock-full of promise. Ranchers know their haystacks are big enough, which balances the red-eyed stare that comes with calving heifers or lambing. That time of year is like watching someone you love begin to stir and stretch before opening her eyes in the morning.

Though I hadn't planned on stopping there, Buffalo presented itself to me about the same time my desire for coffee did. I parked the pickup down the street, and as I walked past the bank on the way to the Bee, I bumped into the same old rancher coming out of the bank and stepping pretty light. Normally, when a rancher leaves a bank, happiness is not your first choice of words to describe him. So I was naturally curious about his attitude. Since he was unarmed and it was still quiet in the bank, I assumed he hadn't shot the banker, which was the only thing that came readily to mind as a reason for his seeming to be so pleased with himself. I suggested coffee and we adjourned to the Bee.

Once we were served, I asked about the smile. "Well," he started in, "you know I had a really good hay crop last year. I didn't have anything to feed it to, so I sold it. Got a good price for it, too. I just took that money in and teased the banker with it and he's lent me enough to go back into the cattle business."

Now I'm really puzzled. This old man is seventy-four years old and he's just borrowed money so that he can spend the winters, when he ought to be sitting next to a fire, out feeding cattle when it's twenty below; so he can lie in mudbanks at two o'clock in the morning pulling calves; so that he can spend the summers bucking hay rather than fishing up in the mountains—all for the privilege of selling cattle at a loss in the fall of the year. I couldn't see why that made him happy. So I asked.

"Don't you see?" he said. "I've won."

"What do you mean, you've won?"

"There's just no way I can live long enough to have to pay this note off at the bank."

There are any number of problems when dealing with the government, but one that seems to be peculiar to rural areas, which means most of the West, hinges on the fact that the twentieth century has not spread evenly over the country. (As an example, I was visiting with a rancher who lives out on the dry side of nowhere when he told me he had been amazed when his neighbor bought a satellite antenna for his TV. "All these years I thought you could get regular radios or big radios with snow," he said. "Now I find out there's pictures that go with those big radios.")

Governments hire people from anywhere, as long as they have the right education and credentials. That often creates problems out here because often these employees don't realize that they've entered a radically different culture from the one they came from.

One common problem is that six-o'clock news-peak hasn't reached out here. We still have regional dialects. People who come out from other parts of the country, especially the more "civilized" parts, often have trouble understanding what's being said.

For instance, the name for a small, flowing body of water, spelled c-r-e-e-k, is pronounced in different ways in different parts of the country. Throughout most of the West it is pronounced *crick*. Not knowing that can create problems.

During the energy boom in the 1970s, some places around the West wound up with more dollars than sense (reading back over that, I realize again the vast difference between telling and writing stories—that's a good pun when you say it, at least when you say it with a Texas accent). Earl Throne of Gillette, Wyoming, told me this story about those days. The fellow he told it on is dead now and can't defend himself, so we'll leave the names out.

County roads are a mixed blessing in the West. The advantage, especially if there's a family with kids past your place, is that the snowplows run on them all winter so the school buses can get around, and you can get into town even when the weather gets bad. The disadvantage is that they aren't fenced, so anyone and his cousin can get onto your place. When you see a vehicle parked on the county road, you have to go check and see what they're doing. The problem is that, as high as the literacy rate is out here, there are people who can't read brands and will occasionally mistake one of your calves for one of theirs and haul it home with them. Surprisingly, people who don't even have brands will sometimes make that mistake.

This old rancher was out riding one day, just checking on things, when he came over a hill and, looking down, saw a pickup stopped on the bridge down on the county road. He figured he better go check, so he trotted down to have a look. As he approached he realized it was worse than he could have imagined; the pickup had government plates. (In places like Wyoming you get in the habit of checking license plates because they tell you not only where someone is from—the number to the left of the bucking horse is the county designation—but how long he's lived there. You get your number in perpetuity, so the longer you've been around, the lower the number. During boom periods it's often important to know whether someone is an old-timer or a newcomer to the area.)

Standing in front of the pickup, with books, maps, and charts spread out all over its hood, was a young man. The old rancher rode up and said, "May I help you?" Now, that question, in that setting, is not really an offer to help. The rough translation is, "What the Sam Hill are you doing on my place?" The kid's response showed he wasn't from that end of the world. He said, "Yes." The young man volunteered that he was there because the government was going to put signs on all the bridges. But, he added, he couldn't find in any of his reference materials what name to put on that bridge. Then he looked all inspired and said, "Say, have you lived here all your life?"

"Not yet," the rancher replied.

Not to be turned aside, the kid continued, "What do you call this?" he swept his arm over the bridge railing.

"Just the crick," the rancher replied, shrugging.

The young government employee thanked him and the old rancher rode off, muttering to himself how thankful he was that it hadn't rained in the last six months. Because if it had rained there would be grass growing on his place. If there was grass growing on the place, the cattle would just naturally eat it. If they ate it, they would gain weight. If they gained weight, there was an off-chance he might make money on them when he sold them in the fall. If he made money on them, he'd have to pay taxes. And he would hate like the devil to have to pay taxes to support the boondoggle project this kid was working on. But since it didn't affect him directly, the rancher forgot all about it in a day or two.

One day, when the rancher hadn't thought about the kid or the signs for a month or six weeks, he and his neighbor were working cattle and rode over the hill that looked down over the county road. There were big new signs at either end of the bridge. The old rancher remembered the kid then, and told his neighbor about the incident. Neither of them had any idea what name would be on the sign—they hadn't, either one of them, lived there over seventy years. So they loped their horses down to take a look. Arriving at the end of the bridge, the old rancher read the sign aloud.

"'Crick Creek,'" he read. "Ain't that just like the government," he said after a long, reflective pause, "the kid got it backwards."

One mark of true maturity is the ability to laugh at yourself. Ranchers must, on the whole, be a very mature people, because often the stories I hear are about the lessons that are hammered home in a fashion that, if you can't laugh at it, you leave.

Lucylle Moon Hall was ranching outside Cody, Wyoming, when I first met her. She was living then on her retirement place—a small ranch, down out of the mountains and only a few miles from town. Lucylle had spent most of her life on a place on Rattlesnake Creek, up in the edge of the Absarokas.

Lucylle's parents had homesteaded on Gooseberry Creek, out in the Big Horn Basin. It was the kind of homestead on which, with plenty of hard work and a good outside job, you could make a living. They determined that their daughter would have a better life. They both worked hard, scrimped and saved, and sent Lucylle to college. She finished school and immediately returned to Wyoming and started ranching. Though she married, her husband didn't like life on the ranch nearly as much as life in the saloons. Lucylle worked the place pretty much on her own, which was okay with her; she liked ranching and was good at it.

Ranching alone, at the end of the road, has some inherent problems. One winter, probably 1936—it was that sort of winter—came a bit before it was expected. Lucylle had a grazing lease on the national forest in the mountains above her place. Her cattle were still up there when a bad storm hit much earlier than usual. The storm dumped enough snow the first night to close the pass for the cattle.

The next day Lucylle gathered her horse herd— packing on some of them a tent, a bedroll, and food for herself and feed for all the horses—and drove the outfit through the pass to the high country. Horses will break a trail through snow that will bog cattle down. She spent the next two or three days riding and gathering cattle. When she had gathered all of them, she packed up her little camp, fed what little feed was left, and headed down the mountain. The snow stopped that day and the horses were able to break the trail for the cattle. But, as often happens when the snow stops, it cleared up and the bottom fell out of the thermometer. Lucylle said she froze up about as bad as you can riding out, floundering through drifts and making sure that everything was following.

As she rode along, doing the work of at least two or three people and freezing in the process, an idea came to her. "Lucylle," she said to herself, "you have a good education. You don't need to do this; you can get any kind of job you want." The more she thought about it, the more sense it made. She could go anywhere and get a good job, make lots of money. And she could work inside where you didn't have to risk frostbite or worse. She could sell this place and go somewhere else to work, somewhere warm.

"We finally got back down below about dark," Lucylle said. "By the time I got everything turned in and fed, and my outfit put away and headed back up to the house, it was probably pushing ten o'clock if not later. I made the mistake of looking at the thermometer as I went into the house. It was thirty below.

"Of course, my husband was in town, had been

since the storm had started, and it was just as cold in the house as it was outside. I got a fire going in the Majestic, put a pot of coffee on, and then sat down in front of the stove with my feet in the oven." (If you've never tried to heat a subzero house with a Majestic cookstove, you've missed one of those occasions that point out the vast difference between an experience you'll always remember and one you'll never be able to forget. It takes a long time just to drive the frost out of the metal of the stove before there's any heat available for little things like the air around it and the coffeepot on top.)

"Finally," Lucylle continued, "it started to warm up a little in the kitchen. My feet started to thaw out from being in the oven, and the coffee started to cook. I began to think of what I'd do with all the money I'd make from my new job and from selling this place. By the time I had my feet back on the floor and my first cup of coffee beginning to warm my insides, I was thinking of the perfect ranch I would buy with my new wealth—how the barn would sit in relation to the house; where the hay meadows would be; exactly how I'd fix it up.

"By the time I was stumping around, getting some food to cook and deciding that my feet weren't a serious medical problem, it dawned on me that I was redesigning this place. Why would I sell this place and go to a city and work just to buy another place like where I was now? I decided to just cut out the middle step and keep this place, it was as nice as any ranch I ever saw and I wasn't ranching to make money, I'as doing it 'cause I loved it.

"Besides," she added with a twinkle in her eyes, "the Depression was on. I probably couldn't have found a decent job anyhow."

Lucylle didn't need another job or another ranch. She kept that one for another forty years, until... But that's a different story.

Drought is a relative term. Anything short of a couple of years is just a *dry spell*. But droughts are a common topic in the West. I spent my formative years during a seven-year drought back in the fifties, a period that is often referred to by folks around there as "the Drought," with a capital *D*, sort of like the Depression.

Drought probably sums up the ranchers' sense of humor about as well as anything. One time I was with a group of ranchers having coffee out in Fort Stockton, Texas, talking about the current drought, when a fellow from back East, visiting one of the ranchers, asked, "Has this drought broke anyone around here yet?"

"No," one of the locals replied, "but we're all bent pretty bad." We all laughed and looked out the window for clouds.

IF IT AIN'T
FATAL...

/V.V.V.V.\

There are those who
figure that all it takes to be a cowboy is to be so
dumb that you can't hold any other job. Those people use the fact that cowboys do difficult, sometimes
dangerous work under conditions that would give
the average OSHA employee a stroke as an example
of true stupidity. I've been around cowboys all my
life and I've only run into one—in life, song, or legend—who was so ignorant that he couldn't even
count. His name was Josh and he used to work for
various members of my family.

I'm sure Josh had ridden past a few schools in his
day, but his shadow had never fallen over the thresh-
old of one. He had not only never learned to read or

write, but had never mastered the art of counting. Oh, Josh could count from one to ten, you just never knew how many numbers he might get in between. That sort of ignorance had never slowed Josh down any as far as handling stock went. He knew horses, mules, and cattle about as well as anyone in those parts, and that was all the education anyone required of him. Not being able to count never caused Josh any trouble, although it created a bit of a problem for Uncle Emzy one time. Uncle Emzy had leased a pretty good-sized pasture that was still stocked, which made the price more attractive. But before he could move any of his cattle into it, he had to get the other cattle out. Before he could do that, he needed to know how many cattle there were, so he would know how much help he'd need to gather the pasture. It was too big and brushy for one man to cover in a day, so Uncle Emzy figured he'd need help to get a good tally. He took Josh along.

Uncle Emzy said they were almost to the place when it dawned on him that Josh wasn't going to be much help in the counting department. Then, as he put it, he had a moment of inspiration. When they got to the gate, Uncle Emzy leaned over and, on the swells of Josh's saddle, scratched some columns with his thumbnail.

"Josh," he told him, pointing to each column in turn, "when you see a cow, make a mark in this column; calves in this one; big steers here; and in this last column for bulls. I'll count the marks when we get back together." They rode off in opposite directions, each covering half the pasture.

Uncle Emzy said they got back to the gate as it was just coming dark. He counted all the marks in the different columns on Josh's saddle, but noticed that Josh had scratched some swirls into the swells just below the columns. When Uncle Emzy asked him about them, Josh replied, "Mr. Emzy, them's bunches."

This story points out not Josh's ignorance but that of those who feel cowboys are. It takes real intelligence to find such a creative solution. And creativity of that sort, coupled with the innate wildness of youth produces much of the humor of the cowboy. It is a humor of youthful exuberance coupled with a protective shield not unlike that of the rancher. Laughing at danger in no way diminishes it, but it greatly lessens the fear attendant upon the danger. As an old cowboy once told me, "Always remember, anything that you can laugh at can't hurt you. It can kill you, but it can't hurt you."

Cowboying is an athletic occupation. The name itself derives from the average age of its original practitioners. Especially back in the open-range days, it was work for youth. A thirty-five- or forty-year-old cowboy was like an aging pro football player of today—much older and more stoved-up than his years would indicate. It's just what happens when you ride bad horses, get kicked by cows, wind up on the bottom of a few bad horse wrecks, sleep on the ground, stay soaked and cold for days at a time, eat bad food seasoned with dust and sand, and cook up skin cancer from constant exposure to the sun and wind. Today it isn't as bad. Most cowboys of today are fifty before they look like open-range cowboys did at thirty-five. But when you're eighteen years old and feel immortal, there is only the joy of being able to do things with and on a horse that separate you, now and forever, from the pedestrians of the world. When you have the world by the tail with a downhill pull, humor tends to aim toward practical jokes. Anything that is not clearly fatal is probably going to be funny. When cowboys get older, they seem not to outgrow the tendency, just to get better at it.

The classic joke of the trail-driving days required a greenhorn, some wet-behind-the-ears kid without a clue about anything. A trail herd had to be watched day and night. While it was drifting along, grazing, riders rode on the flanks and at the lead to keep it pointed in the right direction and at the rear to keep the drags—stragglers—from falling too far behind. At night, while the herd was bedded, one or two riders at a time rode around the herd to watch for signs of trouble that might lead to a stampede. The night watches were usually two hours in duration, everyone taking turns.

Clocks were virtually nonexistent on the open range. Any that were there were unlikely to work for long owing to rain, sweat, dust, and just getting handled a bit rougher than the mechanism was designed for. So night watches were set by the rising or setting of certain constellations. Green kids, as a rule, knew nothing about either the positions of constellations or how long an hour was, as many of them had grown up without clocks, working from daylight till dark and then sleeping all night. So the old-timers would, over supper the first evening, tell stories of their first night watches. Each in turn would tell of how the two-hour watch dragged on for what seemed to be the entire night. Then they would honor the kid by giving him the first watch, solo, unless there were two kids green enough for the trick. The boss would point out the Little Dipper to the kid and tell him to come in and get his relief when it set.

The kid went out to the herd to spend the longest two hours of his life, while the rest of the crew crawled into their blankets for the last uninterrupted night's sleep for the next three months. Along about the time the sky started to turn gray in the east with approaching dawn, the light also began to dawn on the kid that the Little Dipper had only rotated around the North Star and never did, never would, drop below the horizon. By the time the kid crawled into his blankets the next night, he was, if he had learned to laugh at himself, not nearly the kid he had been when he went out to stand his watch the night before. If he woke up the next morning still wanting to climb on a salty horse and ride drag all day, he had the makings of a cowboy and the old hands would start to teach him.

When a cowboy starts to work for an outfit, he is assigned a string of horses. No one tells him anything about them; to do so would be an insult to the cowboy, implying that he needed to be forewarned or he couldn't handle problems the horses might give him.

Time was when every ranch had one or two horses at the far end of the rough string. In fact, there are still more than a few places that have one or two sure-'nough broncs hid out back of the barn. Nobody goes out to his way to ride these horses, but they're there if needed. Their main use these days is being given to new hands to see how good they are, but in the old days they were the means to pull a practical joke when a dude or a braggart showed up.

Good cowboys have always been able to find work once the locals know they are good. Finding a way to demonstrate how good they are when arriving in a new place has often been an exercise in creativity. Creativity, in any field, produces stories. This tale is one I've known about all my life. John Lomax included a version in his collection of cowboy songs early in the century. It is a true story, it must be; I've had the exact place it happened pointed out to me in five different states. That's really the importance of a story like this. Probably something like this happened several times in different places. Naturally people talked about it, and finally the story became well known and widespread enough to be formalized into verse, have music added to it, and become part of our folklore. As folktales and songs drift around through the country, they change to meet local conditions, so the way I learned the story as a kid is a bit different from the version that Lomax recorded. Always, though, the story starts the same.

> *We'as camped out on the plains*
> *At the head of the Cimarron,*
> *When this stranger happens by*
> *And he stops to argue some.*

If It Ain't Fatal...

Well, he looked so very foolish
We commenced to scout around,
'Cause we pegged him for a greenhorn
Who'd just escaped from town.

We asked him if he'd et.
He said he hadn't had a smear.
So we runs him at the chuck box
And bades him take a share.
He helps himself to beefsteak,
To biscuits and to beans,
And then he lights in to talking
About foreign kings and queens.

When he finished eating
And he'd put his plate away,
He helps himself to coffee
And stays to pass the time of day.
Now he could talk about the weather,
The election and such things
But he don't seem to know straight up
About working on the range.

He was such an edjacated feller
His palaver come in herds.
I mean he 'stonished all us punchers
With his big jaw-breaking words.
But, truth is he kept on talking
Till he made us boys all sick,
And we kinda got on the scout
To see if we couldn't pull some kinda trick.

*   *   *

Now, he said he'd lost his job
Up on the Santa Fe
And he's heading 'cross the plains
To join the 7D.
He weren't none too specific,
Something about trouble with his boss.
And then he asks if he can get
A nice, fat saddle horse.

We gets all excited then;
Goes to laughing up our sleeves.
We said, you bet, we got one,
Just as nice and fat as you could please.
Then ol' Shorty he jumps up
And ropes the Zebra Dun.
And we boys all gather 'round
To watch a little fun.

'Cause, you see, the Dun's an outlaw.
He has gone so awful wild
He can paw up moon dust
Every jump for more than a mile.
But while he's being saddled
He stands, like he don't even know.
Though what he is is a trap,
Getting set and waiting for the go.

When that stranger hits the saddle
Ol' Dunny quit the Earth.
He bogged his head, blowed his cork,
And goes for all he's worth.

He was bucking, pitching, squealing,
He was throwing wall-eyed fits,
With his hind feet perpendicular
And his front ones in the bits.

We could see the tops of the mountains
Under Dunny every jump,
But this stranger's camped up on him
Like a gol-danged camel's hump.
I mean he just sat up there on Dunny
And twirled his black mustache,
Just like some city boarder
Who's a-waiting, for his hash.

I mean he'd quirt Dun when he jumped
And he'd spur him when he whirled.
The whole time he's a-grinning down on us
Like he's a wolf of this old world.
Finally, the Dun just had to give it up
And the stranger stepped back down.
By then we know he's a thoroughbred
And not some dude from town.

The boss, he's been a-standing there
Just a-watching all the show.
He kinda sidles up next to the stranger
And says, "You really needn't go,
'Cause if you can rope about half as well
As you just rode the Zebra Dun,
Then you're the man I've been a-looking for
Since the year of one."

Truth is, up next to his roping
His riding's kinda slow,
And whenever we're in a tight
He's always a little extra full of go.
I guess if there's one thing in this world
I've learned in the time since I'as born,
He sure taught me that every edjacated
Fellar ain't a plumb greenhorn.

(I learned this, as a kid, through osmosis by hearing it sung and recited. The Lomax version was first published in 1910.)

The "edjacated feller" of the story, called either "The Zebra Dun" or "The Edjacated Feller" in folk collections, was indeed a top hand who was looking for work in new country. Knowing he would be hired if he could only strut his stuff, he decided to take advantage of the old practical joke of sticking a dude on the worst horse you could find and then watching the fun. There are few things more satisfying than turning the tables on a good practical joke.

When that educated fellow joined the outfit, he joined as cowboys traditionally have—body and soul. Cowboys are as committed to the brand they are riding for as a knight to his king. There's one difference: the cowboy serves at his pleasure as well as the outfit's. If the ranch does not adhere to the unwritten code, the cowboy might leave with no advance notice. Failure of the code might be something as simple as not providing a decent cook, or food for him to work with; or it might be as severe as allowing someone else to ride a horse in the cowboy's string. (That does not sound serious to someone unfamiliar with horses, but since everyone handles them differently, someone else riding a horse that you have trained might well teach the horse a bad habit that you then have to train out of it; or worse, it might do something at a critical moment that you aren't expecting and get you in "a world of hurt.") By the same token, a ranch that did things right could keep good hands indefinitely.

The Eaton brothers ran such an outfit. Because of that, good cowboys kept coming back to work for them year after year. (Cowboying is largely seasonal work; the Eatons would only need a small fraction of the number of cowboys in winter that they would need in summer. In the period we're talking about, the operation was a ranch, a dude ranch—the first ever—an outfitting business, a farm, and a rodeo. It took plenty of good help, and because of the way it was run, it never had trouble getting it.) For instance, Curly Witzel worked for the Eatons, off and on, for seventeen years. Having Curly around was a treat and a challenge; Curly had an active sense of humor.

Curly was one of those rare characters who knows that his life is a story and that it was up to him to make it a good one. He was cowboy, rodeoer, stunt man, silent movie star, pilot, stock detective, wagon boss, ranch foreman, and more. He'd done it all before he hung it up, and he didn't hang it up until he was crowding eighty. He had to quit then because his son, John, was ready to start junior high, and the rural school out where they were living only went through the sixth grade. If you do the math separating Curly's and John's ages, you'll believe any story about Curly. And they're all true.

Curly and Bill Eaton—Big Bill, an obvious nickname for a man Bill Eaton's size— were friends and antagonists. They spent worlds of time pulling practical jokes on one another or teaming up to pull them on others. Not simple, crude ones of no art, but elaborate, elegant jokes to the cowboy mentality. While Curly and I were discussing the art form of the practical joke, he told me that he and Big Bill had become so accustomed to such jokes that they could see one and not have to discuss it before pulling it. As the saying goes, therein lies a story. It started as one joke and stretched, as practical jokes often do, into a series stretching out over a month or more.

One fall, back in the twenties, Bill Eaton bought paint and brushes with a view of having some of the cowboys paint the barn. Unfortunately, all the brushes he purchased were left-handed and the cowboys were all right-handed. By the time spring rolled around, and a blacksmith showed up looking for a horseshoeing job, the barn still needed painting. And Big Bill had a plan.

Eatons', as the ranch is called, must have had close to two hundred fifty horses and mules then. Keeping shoes on them was good steady work, with good food and the benefit of all the young, single women that dude ranches attract—young single women oftentimes smitten with cowboys (and who couldn't tell the difference between a cowboy and a blacksmith). In other words, a job worth doing a little extra to get. Bill knew that and recognized not only a good practical joke but a way to get his barn painted.

The Eatons' dude ranch is in the edge of the Big Horn Mountains above Sheridan, Wyoming. It's not an ideal place to winter horses, so the Eatons have a ranch at Echeta, on Wild Horse Creek, sixty miles out into the Powder River Basin, to winter their horses. When the blacksmith showed up, looking for a job, the horses were still out at Echeta, so Bill told the blacksmith he'd hire him if he'd do general ranch work until the horses came back. Then, before the blacksmith could answer, Bill asked him whether he was right- or left-handed. After the blacksmith agreed to the terms and told Bill that he was right-handed, Bill took him to the barn, the paint, and the right-handed paintbrushes.

The second part of Bill's joke revealed itself in front of the barn. The Eatons hadn't sent all the horses to Echeta for the winter. The ones that had stayed at the ranch had to be fed hay all winter. Like all the ranches back then, and quite a few of them today, Eatons' used a horse-drawn sled for feeding. The two horses that pulled the sled were the only ones that had to work all winter, so they got to spend the nights in the barn and were fed grain. That was good pay for horses, since the nights could hit twenty, thirty, forty, even fifty below outside. The barn, complete with manger and grain box, made having to work all winter a bit easier. Of course, it created a problem; the horses weren't housebroken. The problem was solved with a pitchfork. While the horses were eating breakfast and before they were harnessed, the straw behind the horses, along with anything the horses might have mixed in it, was picked up with the pitchfork and pitched out the door. By the time the horses got back to the barn after feeding, the straw and everything else had frozen. If everyone forgot about it every day for six months, as most cowboys would, the pile out front of the barn was ten or twelve feet in diameter and six or eight feet high. As the spring sun warmed it, first it thawed and then it began to ripen. The rule on Eatons', as on most ranches, was that the first one to complain about the pile got to clean it up. Most of the cowboys avoided the barn in the spring. Bill figured that since the blacksmith couldn't, he would get around to cleaning up the pile before he was done painting the barn.

Give the blacksmith credit, though. He knew how the game was played, and he was not going to give in easily. He painted three sides of the barn, including the trim, before he finally had to deal with the front and the pile. The barn at Eatons', like a lot of old barns, was built so that the ridgepole stuck out several feet in front. There was a hook in the end of the ridgepole so that a block and tackle could be rigged there to lift hay bales up to the loft. The blacksmith had made a scaffold from a couple of boards and some rope run through the block. He was working up near the ridgepole, standing on his scaffold, about eight or ten feet over the pile, painting as fast as a human could paint, trying to breathe every other day, when Curly and Big Bill happened to walk by. The rope from the scaffold ran up through the block and down to a tree stump near the corner of the barn, where it was tied off. Curly said that, as he and Bill walked by, they noticed that, although there was no good reason for it, an ax was leaning against the stump.

Curly said, "I looked at the ax and the stump and then followed the rope from there up through the block and down to the scaffold. Bill had done the same thing. When we noticed that the scaffold was directly over the pile, we looked at each other and smiled. Neither of us said a word. I just took a silver dollar out and flipped it. Bill won the toss, so I stepped back. He picked up the ax, hefted it...and cut the rope.

"It was quite a wreck. Aside from everything else, the blacksmith had just opened a new five-gallon bucket of paint. Trouble was, the blacksmith didn't see the humor in it. There was nothing he could do to Bill, he was a little too big for even a blacksmith to pick a fight with. Besides, Bill could fire him. So he took it out on me."

Within a few days the blacksmith had cleaned up the front of the barn and finished painting it. As soon as he did, the horse herd came in from Echeta (there may have been some correlation there) and everyone turned out to get shoes nailed on a couple of hundred horses before the dudes arrived. Then the ranch went on summer schedule. On a dude ranch, that meant the cowboys and wranglers got up at about four or four-thirty in the morning so that they could get the horses in before breakfast. The blacksmith, since he couldn't go to work until the horses got there, got to sleep in until breakfast. Of course, he was in the same bunkhouse as the others, so they woke him up getting up and out.

Eatons', like all dude ranches, fed in shifts. The help ate first (allowing the guests time to sleep later in the morning, clean up at noon, and have cocktails in the evening), which meant that the cowboys and wranglers had time for a nap after dinner before taking the dudes out for their afternoon ride. Since the blacksmith got to sleep in, he was expected to go right back to work after dinner. This presented him with an opportunity to get back at Curly. He appointed himself the alarm clock for the bunkhouse.

Curly told me he'd be napping just fine when the blacksmith would tiptoe into the bunkhouse, up to Curly's bunk, and tag him one on the arm. Curly said that when the blacksmith hit him, he'd yell loud enough to wake up everybody else in the bunkhouse. (If you ever have the opportunity to be hit by a blacksmith, pass it up; they tend to be fairly well developed through the arms and shoulders.) This went on for nearly a week, and Curly said he was beginning to worry that he might have to apologize to the blacksmith. That went very much against Curly's grain, but he said he could barely raise his arm, it was so sore—the blacksmith hit him in exactly the same spot every time.

"But," Curly said, "before I had to do that, I'as walking up to the bunkhouse one afternoon, and as

I walked past an old buggy, I put my hand on the hub of the rear wheel. It slipped on the axle." I can imagine the smile that came over Curly's face, the barely controlled glee of a practical joker who knows that the wound is going to be far enough away from the heart to be legal. He went on, "The hub was loose enough to work off. I tried it on; just rolled up my sleeve and slid the hub up my arm. It fit just right; right over my bicep where he'd been hitting me. I rolled my sleeve back down over it and went up to take my nap. Let me tell you, it was that black-smith's yell and not mine that woke everybody up that afternoon."

Curly and some of the other cowboys pitched in and helped the blacksmith for a few days, until his hand had healed up. The help healed more wounds than his knocked-down knuckles, and that string of jokes ended.

Today there are plenty of small Western towns that don't have enough traffic and/or money to install traffic lights in their major intersections. Folks from back East are, I think, often surprised to find any at all. They expect the 1890s rather than the 1990s when they get here. (If I had a dollar for every time I've heard someone in Yellowstone tell me that they thought they would be driving through an Indian reservation on their way to the Park, but that they must have missed it and then revealed to me that they came through either the Crow or the Wind River reservation, I'd be rich. They missed it because they were looking for painted people wearing feathers, riding horses, and living in tepees.) But that expectation is not something we can lay on the failure of our education system in the last few years. It's always been that way. The West is our mythic landscape, and people have trouble perceiving myth accurately. The misperception does open up some areas for the quick-thinking, practical-joking cowboy.

In the 1930s, when Curly Witzel was rodeoing pretty seriously, he and Paddy Ryan were running mates. Paddy went on to become the world champion saddle-bronc rider. I don't mean to take anything away from Paddy—he was the best and proved it many times—but I've talked to several folks who knew them both and who said that if Curly had worked at it as hard as Paddy, they would have been pretty evenly matched. This is simply a way of showing you Curly's bona fides.

Another fellow Curly rode with a good deal back then was Bob Crosby, another sure-'nough hand good enough to win it all in Cheyenne a time or two. In 1936, Curly and Crosby decided that they needed to go to what was then the biggest-purse rodeo in the country, held in Madison Square Garden in New York City. The Depression was in full swing, and they figured to make the winter on their winnings. Besides, it would be a great trip. They were both bulldogging as well as riding broncs; the catch was how to get to New York with their horses. Normally a couple of cowboys with horses would contract for an immigrant car on the railroad. An immigrant car was a boxcar modified for people and stock. One end of the car had stalls, mangers, and feed bunks, the other end had bunk beds, a table and chairs, shelves, and a cookstove. Cowboys could stay with and take care of their horses on the trip. But, as I said, the Depression was going strong and Curly and Bob didn't have the money for the train. Crosby did have a Model T, though, and Curly was able to borrow a trailer. They jury-rigged a trailer hitch on the Model T and hooked on the trailer. They tied a couple of bales of hay and a couple of sacks of grain to the back bumper and their saddles to the front fenders. Then all they had to do was load the horses in the trailer, throw their bedrolls and war bags in the backseat, and they were ready to go.

Curly said, "We didn't have a lick of trouble until we hit Chicago. But back then, the main highway going to Chicago was the main street when you got into Chicago. And our timing was perfect; we hit downtown at 5:00 P.M., the middle of the rush hour. I'as amazed that so many people could afford gasoline.

"The traffic, but especially the traffic lights, was causing us problems. You might not be old enough to remember Model Ts, but they were not designed for pulling trailers; they had pretty small four-cylinder engines. And they were designed for the open road; they needed lots of wind blowing through their radiators to keep them cool, something they couldn't get in stop-and-go traffic. When a Model T engine overheated, it stalled and died. You might as well not even have bothered to try cranking it until it cooled off, which could have taken forty-five minutes or an hour.

"Crosby was driving, but I knew we'as in trouble because I could see a little steam ease out from around the radiator cap every once and a while. Finally, Crosby turned to me and said, 'Curly, it's these danged stoplights. If we don't run this car a ways and cool it off, this engine is going to stall on us.' I just looked at him and told him that we couldn't afford to get stuck in downtown Chicago with these two horses, and that he'd better just run the thing a ways and cool it off. By George, he did it. He just took off driving like we were out in the country. We didn't get but about six or eight blocks before a cop stopped us. He pulled us over to the side of the street, pulled his motorcycle up in front of us, got off of it, put it up on its kickstand, walked real slow back to us, put his foot on the running board, and then, before he could say anything, Crosby lit into him.

"'Officer,' Crosby started, 'these are the rudest, nastiest, most reckless drivers I've ever seen anywhere in my life. Why, a half-dozen have almost run into me, and they're yelling things at me I wouldn't yell at an egg-sucking dog.'

"The cop stared at us for some little time before he inquired as to whether or not we had observed all the stop lights.

"Before Crosby could say anything," Curly said, "I kinda ducked my head, so I could get eye contact with him and the cop at the same time, and said, 'See, Bob, I told you those red lights musta meant something.'

"For the first time, I think, the cop really looked at

us. He took in our Stetson hats, our boots, the bedrolls in the backseat, the saddles on the fenders, and, mostly, the horses in the trailer. He took his foot off the running board and walked around to the front of the car and looked at the license plate. That's when he saw what he was up against—1936 was the first year they put the cowboy and bucking horse on the Wyoming license plate. He walked, real slow back around to the driver's door and put his foot back on the running board. I thought we were in serious trouble, but I noticed him cut his eyes around at them two horses before he said anything, and I knew we were all right. He mighta wanted to arrest us, but he knew there wasn't a jail cell in Chicago big enough to hold them two horses. So he just said, 'Follow me.' He got back on his motorcycle, turned on the flashing lights and the siren, and escorted us right through Chicago. He got us to the far side of town and pulled us back over to the side of the road, turned off his flashing light and siren, got off his motorcycle, put it up on the kickstand, and walked, real slow, back to the car. He put his foot back up on the running board and then he just stared at us. And he could stare. We just kept sinking down lower and lower in our seats, trying to hide under our hats.

"Finally he said, 'Where you boys headed?' We told him we were headed to the big rodeo at Madison Square Garden in New York City. He thought about that for a while before he spoke again. 'Well, boys, I wish you lots of luck at the big show, but I've got one piece of advice for you.' We just looked at him and said, 'Yes sir.' 'No matter how you do at the big rodeo,' he told us, 'why don't you go home through Indianapolis.'"

If you believe in practical jokes, as most cowboys do, then I think you must assume that not only everyone but everything believes in them too. Mother Nature is such a practical joker that you have to see the humor in her jokes, even when you're the one she pulls them on.

The tail end of the summer of '71, Butch Swallow and I set up the Triangle X's upper hunting camp, at Phelps Pass. It's a long haul up there, taking from early morning to nearly dark to get there, that time of the year. We pulled into the meadow just as the clouds overflowed and it started to drizzle. We had time to unsaddle, get the cook tent up, cover our gear with manties, picket the bell mare, turn the rest of the stock loose, and get inside before the rain started in earnest. The cook tent was a fourteen-by-eighteen-foot wall tent. We got the kitchen stove up and going, cooked supper, and enjoyed listening to the rain on the canvas while we were dry. We turned in, feeling good about having gotten so much done and about being dry and warm.

About two or two-thirty, I woke up from a dream about being underwater, to find the cold, wet canvas roof of the tent molded to my face. When I finally got reoriented, I crawled out of my bag and out from under the tent. I found myself pretty much as I'd entered the world, but in about eighteen inches of snow. Although it was still snowing hard, I could see clearly because of the full moon behind the clouds. The rain had turned to heavy, wet snow, enough to break the ridgepole of the tent.

I started scouting around for Butch, and found him when one of his hands came up through the snow. It had slipped off the ridgepole he was trying to push off his stomach. The roof had started to leak during the night, and Butch was under a drip. In his efforts to scootch around out from under it, he had wound up under the ridgepole. When it broke, one end of the break had caught Butch in the stomach and pinned him down, inside his sleeping bag. I crawled back under the tent, got under the ridgepole, and was able, pushing with my feet, to help Butch get loose. One corner of the tent was still up, so we dragged our bags into the little cave formed there and went back to sleep.

In the morning we surveyed the situation. After looking things over, Butch informed me that there was only one thing that kept him from catching the horses and leaving: the horses had already left. We still had the bell mare we had picketed, so Butch took her out to bring back a new ridgepole for the cook tent. I pitched one of our eight-by-ten-foot sleeping tents, shoveled the snow out of it, and brought in a stove. I left the fire to dry the tent while I was able to find our kitchen outfit and groceries. By the time Butch got in with the pole, I had breakfast ready in a relatively warm and dry tent.

For two people who were in the running for Most Miserable Human at sunup, we were picking up pretty well by the time we got to our second cup of coffee. We started telling the story to each other and laughing at the storm, the tent, and ourselves. Each time we told it, we thought of more details and laughed harder. When we'd finished the coffee and come out of the tent, the snow didn't seem so bad. We dug through the snow, found all the gear, and got the tents up and stoves into them to dry them. By the time we were finishing up, in the late afternoon, the snow was letting up. Tom Breen and Ric Davis showed up about then with our horses. The horses had stopped at lower camp, where it had only rained, and Ric had caught them for us. We put the coffeepot on and entertained Tom and Ric with stories of our night.

Butch and I had been the butt of one of Mother Nature's jokes, but by laughing at it, and at us, we saved ourselves. We stayed and had a good fall.

Very often, if you can laugh at the jokes people pull on you, they stop pulling them because they aren't as much fun. I think Mother Nature has a little longer attention span than most practical jokers. She must. I've been laughing at her jokes on me for years, and she's still pulling them.

Maybe living close to nature encourages cowboys to think of practical jokes. Maybe the exuberance of youth living a wide-open life encourages practical joking. Maybe it's just that once you start pulling practical jokes, they take on a life of their own and you can't stop them. Maybe it's some of all of those ideas. Whatever the reasons, I see no likelihood that practical jokes will stop being part of cowboy culture anytime soon.

DOWN THE ROAD

.\./\./\./\.

If cowboys love the types of practical jokes described in the last chapter, then you'd expect the games they play to be a bit on the rough side too. They are; and they are known collectively as *rodeo*. There's been enough written about the origin of rodeo that I don't think we need to go into it here. Most rodeo stories that make it into print are either about the history or the great rides and riders. The stories that get told back of the chutes, and over beers or coffee before or after the show, tend to be a bit different. Those stories are about "going down the road," the life of the rodeo cowboy.

There was a time when all cowboys rodeoed some. Today, more than a few ranchers keep a little better roping horse than they might need for day-today work, just for the local ropings every weekend. And of course there are quite a few ranch kids who rodeo a good bit, maybe on the high school or college team. But more and more today, if you want to rodeo seriously, you need to belong to the PRCA, the Professional Rodeo Cowboy Association. That means you need to rodeo for at least several months out of the year. It means you have to travel to a different show each week, maybe more than one. It means you have to go down the road.

Rodeoing today is like cowboying was before barbed wire, a game for kids. Rodeo cowboys are professional athletes, and they last about as long as football or basketball players. The stories told reflect the type of people who rodeo. The sense of humor is similar to that of the cowboy in general, which stands to reason; in spite of their differences from working cowboys, the competitors are still cowboys.

There aren't any teams in professional rodeo, though high schools and colleges do have them. Essentially, rodeo is a group of individuals getting together and betting about who's the best at what he does. You have to pay an entry fee to enter each event, and those fees become the purses to pay off the winners. Learning to rodeo can be really expensive because you can spend a considerable amount in entry fees contributing to the health and well-being of others before you get good enough to begin to win a bit of it back. Even when you're winning, it's hard to make much money rodeoing. Aside from entry fees, there's gas, food, lodging, and so on, that comes out of your pocket while you travel from show to show. That hasn't changed much over time. Back in the 1920s and 1930s Curly Witzel was rodeoing seriously and doing pretty well, but finances could be a problem.

"Paddy Ryan and I were traveling together. We had a car to drive from show to show. We'd ship our horses and pick them up when they got to town. It wasn't any problem in those days to find places to keep horses, and you could pretty well trust the railroads, back then, to get them there on time and in good shape. We'as on our way to Manassa, Colorado, for the Labor Day rodeo. I don't know if you traveled any down there before they reworked those eastern Colorado roads, but back then the landowners had more power at the Capitol than the highway department did. The roads ran along property lines. When they hit a corner and had to turn, the turn was just like a streetcorner, a right-angle turn with no bank. And not much warning before you got to one.

"Paddy and I were arguing as we went along. We'd agreed to pool our winnings in bulldogging to cover expenses, but each of us would keep his bronc-riding winnings. Well, I'd been winning most of the dogging events and Paddy'd been winning most of the saddle-bronc events. I was pointing out that I was supporting him and he was cleaning up as a result. I even suggested that he might not be giving it his all in the bulldogging, saving himself for the broncs. He disagreed.

"Now, it was nighttime, and the more we argued, the faster Paddy drove. It got to where we were taking some of those corners on two wheels. I figured that as long as we were arguing I might as well say something about his driving. When I did, Paddy just stopped the car and said, 'Well, if you don't like the way I drive, maybe we just ought to get out and fight about it.' I said that was fine by me and jumped out of the car. Paddy had left the headlights on so we could see, so I ran around and stood right in front of the bumper. Of course, the old cars' headlights were up at waist level, so when Paddy got there he was looking right into them and couldn't see a thing. I knocked him down. When he got up, he said, 'Fair's fair, Curly. It's my turn to have the headlights.' What could I do? Paddy was my best friend. I let him stand in front of the headlights. Of course, he knocked me down. I got up and we switched places. I knocked Paddy down. And so it went until, after a while, Paddy asked me what we were fighting about. I couldn't remember just at that moment. He couldn't either, so we got back in the car and went on to Manassa."

I told that story one night in Buffalo, Wyoming. Several old friends of Paddy's were in the audience. Two of them came up to me afterwards and told me that they had heard Paddy tell the same story. Except, they said, when Paddy told the story, Curly was driving.

In the West, every town, large or small, has an annual rodeo. Back when Curly and Paddy were rodeoing, quite a few towns didn't have real arenas. I was in the Dubois, Wyoming, museum a few years ago, digging through the accumulated artifacts, photos, and reminiscences of the upper Wind River Valley, when the folks there mentioned that they had a movie they had been able to transfer to safety film, of one of the Dubois rodeos from back in the twenties. They wondered if I'd like to see it. I allowed that I had time.

The Dubois rodeo had gotten fancy by then; they'd built a bucking chute. Before that they'd just snubbed the bronc up to a stout saddle horse and worked in the open getting it saddled and the rider aboard. But with a chute everything could be done easier and safer. They had a bucking chute, but they hadn't built a fence yet. There were several men horseback out in front of the chute a ways to try to turn back the broncs, but that didn't always work. One horse, the rider sitting straight up and spurring, just ignored the horsemen and headed for the mountains with half a dozen dogs encouraging him along. About two horses later, the two returned, the horse running for a ways and then collecting himself and bucking for a while before settling down to run again. The cowboy, quite a bronc stomper, was steering him, as much as possible, by hitting him on the side of the head with his hat. When they got back to the rodeo grounds, the hazers and pickup men finally got the horse surrounded and it stopped. The rider got off, the bronc was led off, and the rodeo continued. At the time we watched the film, no one had been able to identify the rider and we didn't know who won the bronc-riding that afternoon. But from the way that cowboy walked off, I figured he'd earned it.

While rodeo has become more and more organized as time has passed, I'm not sure the cowboys have. Oh, don't get me wrong, there are a few of them who have learned the lessons that other professional athletes have. They've gotten well enough organized to "make it" in their chosen field. But most young cowboys get into rodeoing because they're pretty good athletes and going down the road is fun. They are doing it as an adventure. Often, when they try to get organized and join the modern world, they show themselves to be more in tune with livestock, which they understand as living things, than with things like airplanes, which are just machines.

Clyde Vanvoras told me once that he was flying with a rodeo friend who had a plane:

"There'as four of us headed to Pendleton for the rodeo. Somewhere out over the Great Basin we started having a little trouble with the oil pressure. Now in a plane you don't just stop and put a quart of thirty-weight in and keep checking it until you get where you're going. We landed at a little airport out not too near anywhere at all. It'as the middle of the afternoon, but the mechanic at this little airport told us he wouldn't be able to look at it until the next morning. That just didn't cut it. One of the boys had drawn in the slack the next morning. We needed to get to Pendleton that night.

"'Teddy, over yonder,' the mechanic said, pointing to a fellow sitting over in the shade drinking a Coke. 'He does some charter flying. You might talk to him.'

We did. Old Teddy was pretty comfortable sitting there in the shade drinking his Coke, and didn't seem too inclined to go flying. But after considerable dickering he agreed to take us for a fee that seemed, well, let's just say we weren't going to get that high in his airplane.

"So we're flying along, trying to sleep, 'cause with the ear plugs that you have to have in those little planes, it's too much trouble to talk. I wasn't sleeping too well, though, 'cause I kept looking at the size of the thunderhead up ahead of us. It'as big enough that the top was strung out by the wind, and as the evening progressed, you could see lots of lightning inside it. About good dark, old Teddy announces that we're there and begins to descend for a landing. I'as some relieved that we had gotten there before that thunderstorm. The idea of flying a little plane even close to one of those was not something I relished. We taxied up to right outside the little terminal and Teddy told us, over the roar of his engines, that he wanted to get headed back before that storm got there, so he wasn't even going to kill the engine. We thanked him, paid him, got our gear, and headed into the terminal as he taxied back out onto the runway. You can imagine what we felt like when we walked into the terminal and looked up at the sign on the wall saying 'Welcome to Baker.' That storm was over Pendleton, and the airport there was closed. Teddy just figured that we wouldn't know the difference. I guess he was right. We had to catch a bus the last hundred miles into Pendleton."

* * *

Clyde and his friends might not have been well enough organized to know where they were, but that little misadventure didn't deter any of them from rodeoing. Larry Travis, on the other hand, was turned off the road, but maybe with a little help.

Larry was a student at what was then still Colorado A&M. But he was a far better than average bull rider. He was rodeoing during the summer and cleaning up. When the fall term was ready to start back at Fort Collins, Larry wasn't ready to quit rodeoing. He decided to drop out of school and make it big as a bull rider. The rodeo at Manassa, Colorado, was Labor Day weekend and Larry was headed there rather than to school.

Larry was supposed to ride his bull at about eight o'clock in the morning, during slack, so he figured to get to bed at a reasonable hour. But he figured he'd better stop by the bar for a little visiting first.

"I was standing at the bar having a quiet drink when the fight started. My clue that a fight was beginning was when someone clipped me a good one just back of my left ear. I went down, and before I got to my feet again, I was outside the bar. During that time, everyone in the place had either kicked me, stepped on me, or spilled a drink on me. I needed a drink or two for the pain after that, so I wobbled down to the next bar for some medicine.

"I got out to the arena about seven-thirty the next morning with a double headache, one from the injury and one from the medicine. But I was a classy bull rider, even in a borrowed hat that didn't fit as tight as my own. I rode with loose rowels on my

spurs and worked the bull. [Technically, you don't
have to spur bulls, but if you do, the judges sure
notice it.] I was trying to limber up without having
my head split wide open, when they ran the bulls in.
I looked in the chute at the bull I'd drawn, and went
to check the rules. I'd been under the impression
that the bulls were supposed to be of the domestic
cattle variety. The thing I was looking at in the chute
was clearly crossed with an elephant. I wasn't sure
if there was room for my legs between his sides and
the chute walls. Once I established that indeed I was
supposed to ride it, I started to get ready. But when
I tried to put my bull rope around the bull, it was a
foot and a half short of having the ends touch. [Bull
riders use a flat-braided rope, placed just behind the
bull's shoulder. It is loose, held by the rider's grip.
That requires a rope that will reach around the bull
with at least a couple of feet left over.] While I was
standing there on the chute, astraddle his back, the
bull arched his neck and laid his head back, almost
on his shoulders, and looked up at me. He was not
pleased with me, and I had the clear impression that
he intended to demonstrate just how displeased he
was as soon as possible. I went looking for a longer
bull rope and some baling wire to lock the rowels of
my spurs. When my time came and the gate asked
me if I was ready, I nodded, and that hurt my head.
It split open down to about my navel on the first
jump. The bull and I parted company on the second
one. Before I got back down to the ground, I had
time to decide that education was not such a bad
thing.

"School had already started by the time I got back to Fort Collins, and things were considerably more regimented than they are today. So I got properly dressed up and went for a little visit with the dean of men to see if I could get back into school. To my surprise, there was no problem. The dean explained that my father had called him, before school started, and told him that I had been unavoidably delayed until after Labor Day.

"I knew my daddy knew the rodeo producer well enough to run a little con on me, to rig the draw in the interest of a greater good. I could see him doing that to discourage me from dropping out of school. But I never knew if he would, or could, hire someone to pick a fight with me the night before."

I mentioned Clyde Vanvoras a little bit ago. Clyde was something else. He was one of the best bareback bronc riders of all times. I think he made it to the National Finals eleven times and won twice, quite a record. After he retired he moved to Cody, a good rodeo town, and settled down. He tried ranching a little, worked for the rodeo producer in town (during the summer there's a rodeo seven nights a week in Cody), and owned a share in the Proud Cut Saloon. I spent many a pleasant hour at the Irma visiting with Clyde. Sadly, I'll hear no more of Clyde's stories. He died, suddenly and young, a few years ago. But he'd led the kind of life he enjoyed. Not many can say that, no matter how long they live. It was a life of good stories.

Clyde was born of Greek and Cajun parents pretty

far back in the bayous of Louisiana, and stayed there for about seventeen years. That country, back then, was so isolated that the owls roosted with the chickens and didn't know any better. Most people don't realize it, but that's serious cowboy country. Granted, the cows do have webs between their hooves, the main purpose of shoeing the horses is to provide ballast, and you have to figure that alligators will get some of your calves every year. The country has produced many a good hand. And it produced Clyde. After working around home and trying his hand in some of the little country shows, Clyde went down the road.

"I'as seventeen," Clyde told me, "and about as green as you can be and still remember to breathe on a regular basis. I'as traveling with three other guys who'd all been on the circuit for a few years. I'as smart enough to know how green I was, so I'as treading kinda light so as not to make a fool of myself. Things were going okay until one day we got hungry while we were in a fair-sized town. At that time in my life, I figured that anything bigger than a combination filling station and general store with two or three houses was a fair-sized place. We went into this place that I could tell had something to do with food, because of the smells. We all sat down at a table and this woman came over and gave each of us a glass of water and a piece of paper. I knew what the water was right off, and was smart enough to figure out what the piece of paper was, although I'd never heard of a menu. I mean, after all, there'as a list of foods down one side and a list of prices down

the other. I didn't want any of the others to think I'as
a hick, so I looked down the page until I saw something I recognized and waited.

"In a minute, this woman comes back over and
asks if we're ready to order. We said yes and,
wouldn't you know it, she asks me first. Well, I'as as
cool as you please. I'd seen the guys at the next table
point on that piece of paper to what they were order-
ing, so I pointed and told her what I wanted. I'as
about to breathe a sigh of relief when she said, 'Do
you want soup, juice, or salad?' She said it like it
was one word—one I'd never heard before. So, I just
looked at her really intelligently and said, 'Huh?' I
saw the guys I'as with start to prick their ears, sens-
ing something amiss in the tone of my voice. I knew
I'as on the edge of deep water, you know how cowboys hoorah one another, so I put on my most
sophisticated voice and said, 'I'll have some of that
soup juice.'"

If you're a rodeo fan, you don't need any explanation, but if you aren't, I'll tell you that Cody has the
biggest purse rodeo in the country on the Fourth of
July weekend. In other words, just about every good
rodeo cowboy in the country is there. I was there,
telling lies at the museum. The day folks started
pouring into town for the show, I was at the Irma
Hotel, having a cup of coffee and visiting with Clyde.
I'd laughed at the "soup juice" story when Clyde told
it, but had assumed that it was one of those stories
that was true even though it hadn't really happened.
Then who should come in but the old-timer, no
longer competing but still going to every rodeo he

could get to, just to watch and visit, who had first taken Clyde down the road. Clyde hollered at him and he joined us. When the waitress came back over to the table to see what he wanted, the old cowboy said, "I'll have a cup of coffee. And bring old Clyde there some soup juice."

Maybe Clyde really was that green when he came out of the swamps.

Back when I was guiding for the Triangle X, one of the other guides was a man named Butch Swallow. Jackson Hole was then, and is today, a major center for drug store cowboys. There are plenty of good hands in the valley, but they are outnumbered by the ersatz variety. Butch was a good hand. He was a sure-'nough good guide, knew his way around the mountains, was a good horseman, and, though it wasn't anything he needed in the mountains, knew cattle. Butch wasn't likely to be mistaken for either a real cowboy or a make-believe one when he went to town. Butch got dressed up when he went to town, put on slacks and a white shirt, loafers and a sweater. He could, if you didn't look too closely, pass for civilized. Actually, Butch *was* civilized. As I recollect, he had a double major in business and philosophy (or some such similarly complementary fields), from Montana State. He'd also won the College Rodeo National Finals bull riding in his senior year. Butch wasn't really too easy to slip into a pigeonhole.

It was toward the tail end of the summer, and Butch had shown up to work hunting camp. I was out of the hills for a day and it just happened to be

Saturday. Back then there was a rodeo in Jackson every Saturday night, so after supper we all decided to head into town to see it. Carl, who'd guided with us the year before, had drawn a bull that night, so a group of us, including Butch, wound up visiting back of the chutes. Several friends of Carl had joined the circle. We were standing around talking when the PA announced that there was an extra bull in the chutes. That wasn't an unusual occurrence at the Jackson rodeo. Lots of kids that came out to work in the valley for the summer were smitten with the cowboy image. Riding bulls seemed to be the quintessential macho cowboy thing to do. So, on Wednesday, they'd stop by the office and ante up their entry fee. By Saturday their passion for being the ultimate cowboy was cooling some. When the bulls came into the chutes and the kids would notice that some of the critters measured about half an ax handle between the eyes and that the eyes were not like their old dog's, that's when they began to fade back into the crowd and the producer found himself with an extra bull. That meant that if he could find someone else who wanted it, he could get two entry fees for the one bull, sweetening the pot a bit. The PA asked again if anyone wanted the bull.

"You know," Butch piped up, "I might just do that." All the fellows in the circle who didn't know Butch laughed, and we, with a gleam born of larceny in our eyes, encouraged Butch with things like, "Sure, Butch, you're tough, you could do it." Harold offered to lend Butch his boots; they weren't but half a size or so too big. Carl said Butch could borrow his bull rope. One of the other cowboys let Butch use his spurs. Almost on cue, one of the strangers wondered whether or not Butch could last two jumps. I ventured that I thought maybe Butch just might be able to ride the bull. The stranger suggested that I might put my money where my mouth was. With barely suppressed glee, I reached for my roll and Tommy said he agreed with me. By the time Butch crawled down into the chute, Carl was holding a considerable sum of wagers.

When Butch climbed down on the bull and started to get set, it all of a sudden dawned on those who had bet against him that in spite of being dressed like a dude, Butch was a bull rider. Carl responded with an appropriate quote on fools and their money and said that as a neutral observer, having friends in both camps, he figured that a bad bet was still a legal bet. About then, Butch nodded for the gate and the question became academic. Butch could have spent eight seconds sitting on the fence about as easily. It got pretty quiet, though, while he did it. I don't think most people expected to see someone in a sweater and slacks riding like that. We may not have made a lot of new friends that night, but we left the rodeo with a lot of money, which seemed like a fair trade-off.

Bull riding is probably the most popular spectator event in rodeo. Among the aficionados of rodeo, everyone has a special favorite, but to the general public, bull riding is the current pick. It is also the event most speculated about. While there are exceptions to the rule, like Butch, I have decided, after much research, that the secret to being a good bull rider is in the heel. If you are familiar with anatomy or old songs, you understand that the heel bone is connected to the leg bone and the leg bone is connected to the hip bone. The hip bone's connected to the back bone and the back bone's connected to the neck bone. And in bull riders the neck bone isn't connected to anything.

I was reminded of that anatomy lesson while standing on the chute, astraddle my first bull. It was a good-sized bull, near a ton, although it seemed bigger, and about three-quarters-Brahman. In other words, I was sliding down onto its back behind a hump that looked big enough to rest my chin on. Wayne, an old bull rider who was coaching me some (and, although he didn't realize it, encouraging me to become a storyteller), stopped me. "One last thing about these bremmers," he said, reaching across its back and grabbing a double handful of skin and pulling it over the bull's back, "their skins are kinda loose." I eased down onto the bull, got set, and then felt myself begin to slide off to one side as the skin shifted. I figured that I'd better nod for the gate so that I could at least avoid the embarrassment of falling off inside the chute. Fortunately I was sliding toward the gate so that, when the bull made his first jump, he came back under me. Unfortunately, on his second jump I continued to slide back to the right and he continued to jump to the left. As I came off, he spun, and I realized just how much a rump roast can hurt if it hits you moving fast enough. The best part of the ride was that I landed on my head. I figure that reconnected my neck bone to my head bone because, although I rode a couple more just so I could say I had, I ended my bull-riding career that night.

Rodeoing today is a highly regulated professional sport. For instance, the flank straps on bucking stock are placed there not to get the animals to buck but to cause them all to buck the same way. The straps are like belts that fit too tight. They don't hurt, but they are uncomfortable enough that animals are going to buck anyway, and will buck with a high kick behind. That way, since all the animals buck in the same style, it is easier to score fairly. All the cowboys are required to spur in the same fashion for the same reason.

Back when, it wasn't like that. Each horse bucked in its own style and each rider rode in his own style. It may have been flashier, but it was harder to score fairly. There were also tricks back then that wouldn't be allowed today, even though they were perfectly fair in those days. For instance, Curly Witzel told me that he had one trick that allowed him to ride one bronc every time he drew it:

"I'd seen him buck several times and noticed that he was a spinner. He'd start wheeling around in tight, fast circles to the left until you had to lean into the circle to stay aboard. When he got you leaning in far enough, he'd swap ends and go to spinning the other way. He did it so quick you couldn't recover. You'd be leaning out and you just couldn't get back to him; off you went. I thought about that tactic and what a rider could do about it. I couldn't see a solution for a long time. If you didn't lean into the first spin, you couldn't stay with him, but if you did, he'd get you when he swapped ends. Then I figured it out; the secret was not to let him reverse directions.

"When I finally drew him, I was ready for him. I had a little vise that I could clamp onto the running board of my car. I set my right spur in the vise and used a file to sharpen its rowels. Naturally, I didn't let anybody see me do it, so nobody understood why I was so cocky as my turn came up. They just thought I was trying to build up my courage. When the gate opened for us, that old bronc came out spinning to the left. I leaned into him and reached up with my right foot and kept spurring him on the neck with that sharp spur. He never would turn back into it, so he couldn't swap ends.

"I rode him every time I drew him, and I think I was the only one who did ride him every time I went out with him. The thing that amazed me was that no one ever realized what I'as doing. No one else ever got the book on that horse."

Today just about every horse or bull has a book on it. Cowboys pretty much share their knowledge, and after a year or two on the circuit, stock is pretty well known. If you don't have first-hand experience with a horse, you can almost always find someone who has and who will tell you what the horse is likely to do. Then you just have to be a good enough bronc rider to get the job done.

Early in my brief rodeo career, I drew a bareback horse I knew nothing about, so I asked around. The arena had a high board fence directly across from the chutes, with the stands above it. The book on the horse was that he'd buck straight for the fence, head fake to the right, and, at the last instant, cut back to the left fast enough that, if you didn't lean with him, you'd lose your seat.

When I nodded for the gate, he exploded and headed for the fence, just like the book said. On the last jump before we hit it, he looked to the right, I leaned to the left, and he cut to the right. I had enough rosin in my glove that I maintained my grip and tried to pull myself back onto my seat. Mistake. It was an old fence, without any paint, that had weathered quite a few seasons. My eyebrows got plucked in the cracks and I was pulling splinters out of the inside of my nose for a week or so. Since it's considered bad form to let on to any injuries while you're in the arena, I was lucky enough to come off, finally, facedown and feet first. That way I had enough dirt stuffed up my nose to keep the blood from flowing. I started breathing through my mouth so I wouldn't sneeze and clear the dust plug out.

As I walked back to the chutes, one of the judges told me, "You were still on when the whistle blew, but we figured the fence was holding you on and had to disqualify you." That's when I sneezed.

I guess most sports are hard to describe to those who haven't participated. Rodeo is so far from most people's world that it may be harder to comprehend.

To folks who aren't around horses, intentionally getting on a horse that's going to buck makes as much sense as getting into a plane that's planning to crash. But the feeling when the chute gate opens is not like anything else I've ever experienced. There's a bubble around you and the horse. The crowd vanishes, and you and the horse exist in a private world. If you have the rhythm, time slows down and the sensation beggars description.

When you're young, it's hard to imagine that the pain that goes away in a day or two is going to come back to haunt you in a few years and stay with you from then on. But, especially if you are good at it, I think the injuries are worth it. On a pack trip into the backcountry one time, I had a doctor who specialized in sports medicine. I asked him if he had ever worked on any rodeo cowboys.

"I've looked at X rays of injuries that would have sidelined a football or basketball player for the season if not for his career. When I've gone in to talk to the cowboy about it, he's wanted to know how long it's going to take and whether or not the cast, if one was involved, could be set so that it wouldn't interfere with his performance that weekend. He'd say he'd drawn something that would pay my bill if he could 'just get it rode.' I've never seen anybody like them."

I tend to agree with the doctor. Rodeoers are a special breed, and though some of them have never worked on a ranch, I think they have all earned the name *cowboy*.

COME
TECHNOLOGY

ᜌᜌᜌᜌᜌ

Our world changes, often much faster than some of us do. I'm getting old enough to appreciate that the older you are when a particular change comes along, the harder it is on you. I'm amazed that my typewriter—read *word processor*—remembers not only what I told it the last time I used it, but even what the day is, something I am seldom sure of. But even before I began to personally feel the difficulty of change, I appreciated the stories it produces.

One of the markers I use to judge old people's perspective is the way they answer three simple questions: Can you remember the first time you rode in a car? The first time you talked on a phone? The first time you heard a radio? If they answer *yes* to one or more of these questions, then it is safe to assume that they were born into a different world from the one we now inhabit. They were born into the world of the horse, a world that had existed for several thousand years and that no longer exists because we completely rebuilt the world to accommodate the automobile.

Plenty of folks thought cars were a passing fad when they were first introduced. They waited for people to tire of their new, noisy, smelly toys and park them so they could become chicken coops. Some people simply couldn't figure out cars at all. Still others, including the horsemen of that last generation, refused to give up living flesh that they loved for dead metal that they didn't, no matter how much easier it might make their lives. But the cars came and changed the world, whether or not everyone was ready. Always, though, there was a first; someone in each little community had to break the ice. In doing so, those auto pioneers have provided us with a wealth of stories.

As part of the centennial of Douglas, Wyoming, a few years back, I was helping the students there to do research on the first hundred years of their town. We conducted many memorable interviews, but one in particular illustrates what I'm talking about here. We interviewed a woman whose father had purchased the first car in Douglas.

Her family had a ranch about a day's wagon ride from Douglas. She, her sister, and her brother were all old enough for school, but there was no rural school near their ranch, so her folks had bought a place in town. Every September her mother moved into town with the kids and stayed until school was out in the spring. Her father had too much work to allow him to take off, so the only times he saw his family were Thanksgiving, Christmas, and Easter— the only school holidays long enough for them to go to the ranch.

After a year or two of this, the rancher decided he had to do something about not seeing his kids grow up. He got to reading about cars and figured that was the ticket. As fast as they were, he could go into town on Friday afternoon, pick up the family when the kids got out of school, and be home for supper. They could spend Saturday and Sunday at the ranch, and then Sunday evening he could drive them back to town, spend the night, and go back to the ranch early Monday morning. That way he could see his family at least one or two weekends a month.

So, one fall when the cattle sold well, he hired someone to tend to the place for a few days and boarded the train for Cheyenne, the closest place with a car dealer. He'd done his research and knew what he wanted, but it still took some time. He stayed three days and took driving lessons. When he was ready to go home, the dealer's people helped him load the car onto the train and get it chained down. When he got it to Douglas, there were plenty of folks around the depot to help him get it loose and to push it off the flatcar onto the depot platform. Since that was ramped, he didn't have to start the car then; they just rolled it down the ramp and parked it next to the station. He covered it with a wagon sheet and went home for supper.

It just so happened that he got home on a Friday night, so they were up, packed, had eaten breakfast, and were down at the depot by the time the sun was cracking the horizon the next morning. But they weren't the only ones there. I'll let the lady from Douglas take up the account:

"There must have been a couple of hundred people there, and more were coming all the time. Everyone wanted to see the automobile. Daddy got the tarp off and we saw the car for the first time. It was beautiful! All black and shiny, and huge. It was a touring car and the top was down. It looked a block long. We got the suitcases in the back and we climbed in. Then I started getting embarrassed because Daddy started talking to himself, out loud."

What he was talking about was all he had to do to get the car started. Back then you didn't just jump in and turn the key. He had to talk himself through getting in, setting the hand brake, getting the transmission in neutral, setting the spark, and adjusting the throttle. Then he got out and went around to the front of the car to crank it, remembered the crank, and talked to himself about where it was as he came around to find it. He found it under the seat and went back around to crank the engine. He reminded himself how to hold the crank so that he wouldn't break his thumb if the engine backfired. He got it cranked and came back around to get in, remembered the crank, and went back for it. Finally he got in, talked himself through getting everything reset, and backed out into the street without either running over someone or killing the engine.

"I was so embarrassed by then," she continued, "that I was sunk as low as I could get in the seat, knowing that I'd never be able to come back to town; everyone would think Daddy was crazy, talking to himself that way. But as we drove along down the street, slowly enough that everyone was walking along with us, it was like a parade. Everyone in town was there by then, and I started seeing my school friends turning green with envy. I got over being embarrassed then. I started sitting up straight and waving to everyone.

"The parade ended at the edge of town, when we crossed the river. The bridge seemed narrower than I remembered it, but Daddy could steer that car just fine. We crossed the river, looked back, waved at everyone again, and headed for the ranch. It was amazing. We were sailing along across the prairie with a big roostertail of dust up behind us. We must have been doing thirty or thirty-five miles an hour."

Now I know that doesn't sound very fast nowadays, but thirty miles *a day* was good time in a wagon. There's also the road. I've been out to her ranch, and thirty miles an hour is still good time on that road. It's just a dirt one, recognizable mostly because there's less grass and sagebrush on it than on either side of it. The big difference in the road between then and now is that now where a fence crosses it there's a cattle guard. Cattle guards, if you aren't familiar with them, are pits across the road covered by a set of rails with gaps between them. Livestock won't, can't get across. Back in those days there were no cattle guards; they weren't invented until after the car came along. Back then there were gates, usually wire gates, where fences crossed roads.

"We went through the first gate, which was closed, at about thirty-five miles an hour, with Daddy pulling back on the steering wheel and screaming 'Whoa!' at the top of his lungs."

We laugh at such a story, but it was not unusual. People had been stopping wagons for centuries with a "Whoa." Ike Breen, who was the foreman of the Triangle X while I worked there, said his daddy had bought the first car in Montana's Judith Basin and had done the same thing. He drove the car home and hollered "Whoa!" as he went into the barn with it. It was a good, solid log barn. They stopped when they got to the back wall. He climbed out and announced that he wouldn't drive anything that wouldn't stop when you told it to. The car sat there until Ike got old enough to get interested in it. He chased out the chickens that were roosting in it, figured out how it worked by cleaning it up, and then fixed it so it would run again. Ike became an accomplished driver and mechanic. His father stuck to horses.

It was no different in Taylor. Mendel Booth was the banker, so naturally he got the first car. It was an important status symbol. Owning the bank in a small town would seem to imply a sufficiency of status, but you know how it is—that's one of those things that, if it's important to you, you can't get too much of.

Everyone in Taylor liked Mendel, which is a high compliment to anyone, but especially to a small-town banker. Mendel was small of stature, though he had increased his acreage as he grew older. The growth had not deepened his voice any; he spoke in high-pitched tones. Maybe he felt the need for status more than some would have. I suspect, however, that he may have lost some of the car's inherent status the first day he drove it.

Mendel drove past the bank and everyone, hearing the new car, came out to see it. Mendel drove around the block and came back by, honking, hollering, and waving. Since no one could hear his voice over the car, they hollered and waved back.

The third time around the block, folks began to suspect that something was amiss, but no one could understand Mendel over the sound of the car. The next time around, someone ran out and jumped on the running board. He discovered and shouted to the others that Mendel had no idea how to get the car stopped. Neither, of course, did anyone else in town. After a half-dozen trips around the block, there were twelve or fifteen men either in or on the car with Mendel. No one had a clue what to do, but that has never stayed men from making suggestions.

When someone accidentally did get the car stopped, no one knew which, of all the things they'd tried, had done the job. The only thing to do was to leave it sitting there, in the middle of Main Street. In a couple of days someone came into town on the train who knew something about cars. Mendel hired him to stay for a few days and give him driving lessons. Maybe that's how chauffeurs became a status symbol in the first place.

Not all driving lessons, back in those early days of the car, were given by drivers to nondrivers. Daddy told me this story of such a lesson. It would have happened sometime during the summer of '26 or '27, a year or two after he finished college.

"I was working around the barn one afternoon when Uncle Emzy came up driving a young horse hitched to a light rig. He had that horse stepping out, coming up from the road. He pulled up and called to me to get my car. I knew enough not to ask questions when he was in a mood like that, so I went to get the Model T. By the time I got it started and back over to the barn with it, Uncle Emzy had pulled the harness off the horse, and turned it into a dry lot to cool off. He climbed into the car and told me to cut through the fields and stop at his house."

Uncle Emzy's house was only about a mile and a half from our place if you followed the turnrows through the fields. Along the road it was over twice as far. In a Model T you could drive just about as fast on the turnrows.

"When we got there, Uncle Emzy jumped out and told me not to kill the engine. When he came back out of the house a minute or two later, I knew there was going to be trouble. He was wearing a coat. I was sure he had a six-shooter under it. He got in and said, 'Let's go to town, quick.

"Going up the hill just the other side of Brown's

Gin, we caught up with a truck. Uncle Emzy told me to pass it, which I had figured to do since it was laboring to get up the grade. But when we passed it, Uncle Emzy told me to stop. I told him that if I did, the truck couldn't get around me and would have to stop too. If it stopped, it'd have to roll back down the hill and try again because it wouldn't be able to pull the hill from a standing start. That didn't seem to bother Uncle Emzy too much. I stopped.

"The truckdriver was pretty upset at being stopped, but before he could set his brakes and get out, Uncle Emzy was climbing up on his running board. He reached up under his coat, pulled out the six-shooter, and inserted about a quarter inch of the barrel into one of the truck driver's nostrils. I couldn't hear what Uncle Emzy was saying but I could tell that the driver was paying real close attention to whatever it was.

"When he finished talking, that fellow nodded a couple of times and Uncle Emzy removed the six-shooter, put it back under his coat and got back into the car. All he said was, 'Let's go home.'

"I was more than a little curious, but I knew enough not to say anything. We stopped at Uncle Emzy's house, he went in and came back out in a minute without his coat. We came on back home. When we got here, Uncle Emzy caught and watered his horse while I put the car away. When I got back to the barn, he was just finishing harnessing. He got in the rig and, before he left, turned to me and said, 'I bet it's a long time before that sorry so and so honks his horn at a young horse again.'"

* * *

Back in the horse-and-buggy days, most people figured that if you had enough larceny in your soul, you could become a horse trader. Now, I don't want to give the impression that all horse traders were crooked, but enough were to enter the folklore as such. Many people figure that the descendants of those horse traders became used-car salesmen. Be that as it may, the first car salesman in Taylor certainly had the genes of a horse trader.

The car dealer was having trouble getting people to buy his cars. Most people figured that cars, even if they weren't just toys, weren't powerful enough to be of any real use around there—the mud gets pretty bad at times. (They were, of course, right. Until the roads were paved, many were impassable after a rain.) Someone suggested to the dealer, probably as a joke, that if he could sell a car to Mr. Kennedy, people might begin to take cars seriously. Mr. Kennedy lived at the top of a steep hill—one of the steepest hills in those parts—just south of Brushy Creek, two or three miles above our place. His fields were down in the bottom, but his house was at the top of the hill. No one figured cars' engines were powerful enough at that time to pull the hill. They also figured that Mr. Kennedy was too tight to spend money on something trivial.

After quietly going out to check the hill in question, the dealer was inclined to agree. But he had figured there would be problems in getting his business started, so he took it on as a challenge. After a bit of thought, he came up with a scheme that would have made a horse trader proud. He went out to talk to Mr. Kennedy. Parking one of his new cars on the side of the road down in the brush along the creek, he slipped up to watch Mr. Kennedy plowing. That allowed him to time his arrival so that he stopped at the edge of the field as Mr. Kennedy turned his mules. Plowing in heavy soil like that, you need to stop for a minute or two and let your mules blow at the end of each row, so the dealer had a chance to engage him in conversation. He complimented Mr. Kennedy on his mules, his farm, and his high standing in the community. Then he suggested that Mr. Kennedy should have a fine car, like the one he was driving, so that people would know what an important man he was.

Flattery works, even if the recipient knows it's flattery, so long as the recipient agrees with it. Mr. Kennedy was flattered, but he was no fool. He looked the dealer in the eye and told him that he would never buy a car because a car couldn't get up the hill to his house. His eyes weren't good enough to see the twinkle in the dealer's eyes then.

"Why, Mr. Kennedy," the dealer said, sounding offended, "this automobile is so powerful it would back up that hill." He counted—rightly, as it turned out—on Mr. Kennedy not knowing anything about cars. That car was geared considerably lower in reverse than it was in first. He backed it up the hill.

Within a week, Mr. Kennedy had bought a car. Within a couple of months he had built a garage at the foot of the hill; the car wouldn't go up the hill forward, and he wasn't a good enough driver to get up the hill in reverse. The dealer stayed in Taylor and made such a success of his dealership that others took up the trade. I know most of them and like them enough not to make any comments about whether or not they copied his style.

The automobile has changed our world more than any other single thing in the twentieth century, I venture to say. But it wasn't the only change that folks had trouble adapting to. Take the telephone—please. It may be the greatest plague on privacy, peace, and quiet in our lives. Yet, used properly, it can make life easier.

When phones first came out, they were sold as labor-saving devices. There are stories that you can never quite pin down as to exactly where, exactly when, and exactly to whom they happened. But if they didn't, they should have. There's one of those about the early ideas about phones.

Back in those days, grocery stores delivered. You could stop by the store and leave a list, and they would deliver the groceries to your house if you weren't able to take them with you. A phone system was being installed in the community, and the grocery store was getting a phone to take orders. There was an old gentleman, one of the generation that wasn't getting along too well with all the newfangled gadgets, who didn't see much sense in having a phone. Some friends suggested that, since he was getting older and couldn't get around as well as he used to, he get a phone. When he asked why, they told him that he could order his groceries and have them delivered. He laughed and said he knew they were pulling his leg. As he put it, "There's no way they could deliver a slab of bacon through one of those little wires."

Some people adapted to the changing times because they had to. Uncle Dud was sheriff of Pecos County, Texas, and had to learn to drive and use modern communication tools. He claimed that he had one of the first police high-speed communication systems in the West. Pecos County, like most parts of the rural West, installed its first phone lines by insulating the staples that attached the top wire of the fences to the posts, and using the fence wires as phone lines. Reception wasn't too good on the party lines when little birds were flocking and using the fences as perches. With a few hundred birds on the line and a half-dozen people listening in, you often couldn't hear much of a conversation.

I'm sure you've seen the phones of that era—big, bulky affairs, wooden boxes with separate ear- and mouthpieces and a crank on the side. If you ever looked inside one, which you probably have if you're a fisherman anywhere in the South, you've noticed that there's a fair-sized generator in there (that's what the crank's for) to get the system on line.

Uncle Dud stuck one of those in his buggy. The wires coming off the phone were only a few feet long, with alligator clips on the ends. All he had to do was pull up next to a fence, clip the wires onto the top wire, and crank onto the party line. In those days before radio, everyone listened in on the party line to keep track of the local news, so he could get a message to just about anyone he needed to. Once he even got an unexpected result from such a call.

Uncle Dud was after a fellow wanted for robbery. He didn't have much chance of catching up with him because of the start the robber had, but he was in his buckboard. He stopped at the first phone fence he came to, and got onto the party line to call Charlie Witcher, one of his ex-deputies who was cowboying on a ranch in the direction the robber was headed. Uncle Dud figured the fellow would have to stop at a certain windmill for water, and Witcher could ambush and capture him there.

Witcher informed Uncle Dud that when he had married, he had promised his wife to completely retire from working as a lawman. Before Uncle Dud could begin to try to persuade him to capture the robber, another voice broke in on the phone and offered to ambush the bandit. Uncle Dud said the voice, even over the phone line, sounded not only sincere but competent. Uncle Dud told the young cowboy to go ahead and try.

Uncle Dud always had good horses, and the two hitched to the buckboard could step out when he asked them to. He asked them to that day. But he was still several miles from the windmill when he met the young cowboy from the telephone, riding behind the robber. The outlaw's hands were tied and the cowboy was looking proud and as competent as he had sounded over the phone. While Uncle Dud took charge of the prisoner, he visited some with the cowboy. The more they talked, the more Uncle Dud liked him. He would have offered him a job, but his staff was full. Instead he offered to talk to an old friend of his, now a captain in the Texas Rangers, to see if there was a chance of the cowboy joining the Rangers. There was, and he did. His name was Frank Hamer, and he became one of the best Rangers of the century, probably best known for tracking down and killing Bonnie and Clyde. That may have been one of the most fortuitous cases of eavesdropping on the party line I've ever heard of.

Some people refuse to adapt to modern times, or at least put it off as long as possible. When western Kansas was finally invaded and conquered by the plow in the teens, Ernest Reese didn't want to have anything to do with farming. He cinched his saddle around his bedroll, threw it on a train, and jumped on after it. When the train stopped for water at Echeta, Wyoming, he got off, caught the next train back to Gillette, and got a job in the saddle shop. Once he got acquainted around Campbell County, he started cowboying and getting to know the country. He wound up with a homestead in the breaks north of Echeta. In later years he added another ranch on Clear Creek, forty miles west.

When he was an old man, still ranching, someone asked him what had possessed him to get off the train at a place as remote and rough as Echeta. He surveyed the breaks and clinker hills with the occasional juniper dotting the canyons. He also saw the wonderful, hardy grasses growing there, which perhaps the questioner had missed. Taking it all in, one of the most subtly beautiful places on Earth, he answered,

"Because I knew they'd never be able to bring tractors into this country." He wasn't far wrong. Ernest died of a heart attack in the fall of '75. He was in his corrals; he and his kids had just finished loading out the last of that year's calves.

Though Ernest had made some accommodations to the twentieth century—he even acquired a tractor before he died, so that he could put up a little hay for his cattle—he had done so grudgingly. He was a horseman of the old school. And he bred true. Dixie and Richard, his daughter and son, share ownership of the two ranches he started.

I mentioned western Kansas getting plowed up in the teens. There was a reason for it. World War I started in August of 1914. By the spring of 1915, just about every farmer in Europe was in somebody or another's army. Not much wheat got planted. But there was still quite a demand for bread. The wheat market boomed. A great deal of the western United States got plowed up to plant wheat between then and 1919. (Though it has nothing to do with this story, a great deal of Argentina, South Africa, and Australia got plowed up at the same time for the same reason. That's just one of those stray bits of trivia I throw in every once and a while so that you can impress your friends or so you can feel like you're learning something from reading this book.)

All that farming created some problems. Not the sort of real problems that the Dust Bowl pointed out a few years later, but immediate problems. The kind of problems that people notice and try to correct. In other words, the kind of problems that affect their pocketbooks right away.

Wheat farming had always been labor-intensive. It took a crowd of people to cut and thresh wheat. There had never been big crowds of people out West. When the war started, the United States was providing more than wheat to the belligerents. Business was booming back east. Everyone without a good job or a place of his own headed back there to make good wages in war industries. Folks with plenty of land to plow didn't have enough help to do their farming. The solution was as close as a catalog. The twentieth century had arrived in their mailboxes. Labor-saving devices had come to the farm—tractors, combines, swathers, threshers, all driven by that marvel of the new age, the internal combustion engine. Now the few could do the work of many. That is, until one of these wonders of the new age broke down. The one thing you couldn't get from either Sears, Roebuck, or "Monkey Wards" was a mechanic. And most of the ones who had been out here had gone east to make really good money in the war industries.

Crisis does, however, offer opportunity for some. Cowboying had always been seasonal work, plenty to do in the spring and fall, not much in the summer, and very little if anything in the winter. So quite a few enterprising young cowboys found that they could get jobs by claiming to be mechanics as well as cowboys. With luck you might get to cowboy for months before something broke down that required you to back up the claim. One fellow did some research before he went looking for a job. As he put it, that helped, for a while.

"I'd found this outfit that was farming a good bit of land but still doing all the work with horse-drawn equipment. Now any blacksmith could fix that stuff, and there was a pretty good blacksmith on the place. The thresher was the only piece of equipment with an internal combustion engine; it was an old steam thresher that had been converted to gasoline. The blacksmith was an older fellow who knew nothing about gasoline engines and didn't want to learn. That left an opening.

"I showed up right after threshing season and asked for a job. They told me they weren't hiring any cowboys then, so I told them I was a mechanic too. They hired me and I got to work the better part of a year as a cowboy. Of course, threshing season did eventually roll around, and the boss told me to go get the thresher running.

"The catch was that there wasn't a big enough shed on the place to hold it, so they'd left the thresher parked out at the edge of a field at the end of the season the year before. The boss had told some old cowboy to cover the engine with a wagon sheet. The cowboy knew less about engines than the blacksmith, and had even less desire to learn. He did know, however, that it would ruin a wagon sheet to leave it out all winter, and he didn't want to be held responsible for that, so he covered the engine with an old one.

"By February the only things left of that wagon

sheet were the brass grommets at the corners. So the last few storms of the winter hit the engine and then some birds nested in it in the spring. By the time threshing season rolled around, that engine needed some expert attention. It took me three days to take it apart, clean it, and put it back together. I figured it ought to work then because there weren't but three or four pieces left over, and none of them looked very important. So the next day I got one of my buddies to ride up there with me to get it started.

"We went up horseback, of course, and carried a can of gasoline along. We filled the gas tank, primed the carburetor, and started in cranking. The engine was one of the old hand-cranked types, and we cranked until we were blue in the face without ever getting that engine to turn over.

"After what seemed like an hour, I took a break to catch my breath and let my buddy crank a while. I'as bent over with my hands on my knees, trying to breathe, when I got to looking at my horse. I'll admit I wasn't much of a mechanic, but I'as a good cowboy and it doesn't set well with me for me to be breaking sweat while my horse is eating grass. I figured if I'as working, he ought to be working too. But there's no way he could grip that crank.

"But, as I'm looking, I notice that my buddy and I are both packing about forty-five or fifty-foot ropes and that engine's got a big flywheel on it. What few engines I'd really worked on before that were little bitty ones that started with pull cords, kinda like lawnmowers do today. I kept thinking about that as

I looked from my horse to the flywheel to the ropes. Finally I figured why not, nothing else had worked, it'as worth a try.

"I tied the two ropes together and wrapped them around the flywheel. Then I cinched my saddle up good and tight, took a couple of dallies around the horn with the end of the rope, hooked my spurs into the horse, and away we went. By George, it worked just as slick as you please. That engine just fired right up.

"You know, maybe I shouldn't have tied that rope hard and fast to the flywheel, 'cause when that engine fired and that flywheel started cranking back, it sucked my dallies down tight and they bound on my saddle horn. I couldn't get them loose. Now I'd roped lots of big things on that old horse, and when something pulled on him, he just swelled up and leaned into it. I don't guess that tug-of-war between the engine and my horse could have lasted more than a second or a second and a half, but when you're about to die, time slows way down. It sure seemed like a long time before the cinches broke on that saddle, but when they did, everything happened in a hurry. My horse headed home without me, and me and that saddle headed back to the engine. Let me tell you, for sixty, eighty feet there, it'as quite a ride too. I'as screaming at my buddy to shut the thing off, but he's laughing too hard to do anything. I finally got shucked of that saddle just before we got to the engine, but before I could get up and dig enough dirt outta my eyes to see which way to face to turn the thing off, it had beat my saddle to pieces, slinging it around, banging it into the thresher, the ground, the engine, and maybe even me a time or two; there were a couple of lumps the next day that I couldn't account for any other way.

"There I was. My horse had gone home without me. My saddle was torn all to pieces. Both ropes were chewed up. And, worst of all, there'd been a witness to the whole thing. The ranch had just gotten on the phone and I figured everyone on the party line would know about it by tonight and the rest of the county by the end of the week. Then, just to add insult to injury, when we got everything untangled and tried to crank the motor again, the danged thing still wouldn't start."

The old man sat there for a few seconds, took another swig of coffee, and looked up at the ceiling. "You know," he said to no one in particular, "I've never been able to get a job as a mechanic anywhere in this county since then."

There always have been new technologies coming along, and I guess there always will be. Once horsemen were the cutting edge of a new technology, but that was long, long ago. Young people always seem to take to new gadgets or new ways better, perhaps because the whole world is new to them, perhaps because their parents don't. But always there are those who have trouble.

When I'm in my eighties, some young storyteller will tell people that one of the markers he uses to tell whether people were born into the old world or the new is whether or not they can remember the first time they used a computer. Like them or not, computers are going to affect our world in the same way the automobile has. It may not be the best news if you're older, but it is creating a whole new cycle of stories. Our children and grandchildren will tell them with the same disbelief with which we of the automobile age tell the stories of the people who couldn't figure out how to make a car stop.

LAW AND ORDER,
MORE OR LESS

∧∧∧∧∧

If civilization is indeed a thin veneer over wilderness, then there were certainly times when it was best applied by someone onto whom the veneer was not too tightly glued. I grew up in Williamson County, Texas, named for Judge Robert M. Williamson. "Three-Legged Willie," as the judge was known, had suffered some disease that had left one leg permanently drawn back at the knee. Unable to straighten it, he wore a wooden leg. Standing, his leg stuck out behind, sitting, the wooden leg stuck out in front. The judge was a civilized man—linguist, jurist, journalist, newspaper editor and publisher, and one of the first judges of the Republic of Texas. But "Three-Legged Willie" was no fop. He'd been a mover and shaker in the revolutionary movement to free Texas from Mexico, and not only as a journalist and spokesman; he'd killed men with rifle and bowie knife at San Jacinto. He was, in the vernacular of the peasantry, someone who could crack his own pecans.

President Houston knew people. He made sure that Williamson was elected judge to a huge district in deep East Texas, Shelby County included. Deep East Texas is part of the Deep South, back then populated by a preponderance of people of old Anglo-Saxon stock who figured they didn't need any outside help to settle their personal problems. In other words, they were feuding stock. Shelby County was the center of a little misunderstanding referred to as the "Regulator and Moderator War." There had been a considerable amount of regulating and moderating going on, with rifles and shotguns, but mostly with the weapon of choice in that part of the world, the bowie knife.

Williamson went there to hold court. On the morning court was to convene, there was a considerable crowd in town, there to see the show, not to see a court session. "Three-Legged Willie" arrived in the courthouse, an empty log building that he had had furnished with a single table and chair. He was impeccably dressed in a broad-brimmed black hat above a frock coat over a clean white shirt and black tie. His high-topped black boot, with a striped trouser leg tucked into it, was shiny and his wooden-leg was oiled and polished. There was a big crowd outside, and the building was crammed with people.

Williamson proceeded to the table and set up shop,

placing his papers on it and sitting down behind it. When he looked up and surveyed the room, he noticed that there were bowie knives aplenty in evidence. A spokesman for the citizenry stepped up to the "bench" and informed the judge that there would be no court held in Shelby County.

"Around here, Judge, this is the law," the spokesman said, laying a bowie knife down quietly on Williamson's papers. Williamson looked the man dead in the eyes and then shifted his gaze to take in the entire room, every man obviously in agreement with the spokesman. He then reached down under his frock coat, with both hands, and produced a brace of Colonel Colt's newly patented Equalizers. No one in that part of the country had seen one before, but most had probably heard of them, and everyone in the room certainly recognized the look in Williamson's eyes. He quietly laid one of the six-shooters on top of the bowie knife.

"That may be the law around here," the judge said, touching the bowie knife with the barrel of the pistol he still held, "but this," now tapping the six-shooter that lay on top of it, "is the constitution of the Republic of Texas. Court's in session."

The story above is not only true but quite possibly factual. It illustrates a point about not only our history but about our Western myth. Colonel Colt did revolutionize the West historically, but he also revolutionized the American myth. The cowboy of myth would not exist without the six-shooter. There is a made-up story, a mythic tale if you will, to compare with the "Three-Legged Willie" story:

In a small town on a Saturday in the fall of the year, when the weather had cooled enough to make everyone want to stay indoors, the saloon began filling early and by the evening was crowded. Smoke hung heavy in the air. The quiet murmur of conversation was mixed with the clinking of chips at the gaming tables—the pleasant buzz of a saloon. Into this peaceful scene a giant of a man entered through the swinging doors. He surveyed the room and saw that there was no room at the bar. Picking out the smallest man there, he walked up to him, seized him by the shoulder, and pulled him away from the bar, saying, "Step aside, little fellow, and make room for a real man." The little man looked up at the giant, nearly twice his size, standing at his place at the bar. He waited for the bartender to serve the big man and then tapped him on the shoulder. The big man turned around, glared down at the little man, and said, "What do you want?"

The little man smiled pleasantly at the giant and said, as though lecturing to a slow student, "When God made men, He made some men big and He made some men little." Then with a movement faster than the eye could comprehend, he had a six-shooter pressed into the giant's midsection. "But when Colonel Colt made his pistol, all men became equal. Now get away from my spot at the bar." The big man moved.

The six-shooter is associated with cowboys in myth, but among themselves, as I've noted before, there are more stories of the cowboy's sense of humor as a way to resolve problems. I've heard the following story, for instance, associated with a variety of settings; some of the tellers have even sworn that we were sitting in the exact place it happened. Exact places are, I tend to discover, seldom very exact.

In one of those towns that sprang up throughout the West in the last century at the "end of all creation," the saloon was packed to the rafters with men simply relaxing and enjoying themselves when the local bully walked in, not through the swinging doors but through the plate-glass window. As if that act hadn't drawn any attention to him, he jerked two six-shooters from his belt and fired a shot into the ceiling.

"I'll give every SOB in here ten seconds to clear out," he roared into the silence following his entrance. Nine seconds later, with the exception of two or three bodies trampled near the door, he seemed to be left alone to drink in private. But, as he surveyed his handiwork, he realized that he was not alone. Sitting alone at a table against one wall was a small, meek-looking cowboy, sipping a beer.

The bully advanced on the table with steam issuing from his ears. Sticking one pistol into his belt, he drove a fist through the tabletop and slung the table off to one side so that he could stand over the seated stranger. The meek little cowboy simply lifted his beer to prevent its being spilled.

"I thought I told every SOB to get out of here," the bully, foam flecking his lips, roared at the stranger.

The little cowboy pushed his hat back, looked up at the bully, and smiled. "Yes sir," he said, "and there certainly were a lot of them, weren't there?"

* * *

Humor may have been as important as the six-shooter to the cowboy in reality but certainly, you think, not in the myth. The Code of the West demanded that you meet your enemy in a fair fight, face to face on Main Street at high noon, the quickest draw and the surest shot proving himself the better man. Yes, the Code demanded that in the movies. In reality the Code of the West was a bit more mundane. It governed day-to-day life in a wide-open country that the laws of the land had not caught up with. The Code may not have provided law, but it did provide order. It dictated simple courtesies, such as how close horses could come to a chuck wagon; as the chuck wagon cook might put it, "You don't ride your horse into your momma's kitchen, you don't ride it into mine."

The Old West was a place where vast distances and a scattered population made the law a spotty proposition. The Code did address behavior to prevent misunderstandings that could result in violence. For instance, it was the height of rudeness to approach a stranger without declaring your intentions. Uncle Bob told Daddy that he and Uncle Frate were headed down to the Post Oaks one time when they saw a man ahead riding parallel to the road and about a half-mile off to one side of it.

"We'as both riding good horses. [That goes without saying with those two legendary horsemen.] We'as out in that good open country, along in there north of Elgin. There weren't any fences back in those days, the road just headed down the country, following the lay of the land. It'as good footing, so we'd let our horses out into an easy lope.

"When we spotted that fellow, we figured that he didn't really want to be seen up close, that he was on the dodge. I suggested that we might just throw a fright into the man by heading toward him. So when we got even with him, we turned and headed right for him. We were still loping and he was just walking his horse.

"As soon as we started toward him, he looked around at us. He watched for a few seconds, to make sure that we were indeed headed for him, and then waved us back. We laughed and kept on toward him, anxious to see what he'd do. He watched us for another few seconds and then stepped off his horse on the off side, so it was between him and us, and pulled a Winchester out of his saddle boot.

"Frate looked at me and suggested that maybe we'd scared that fellow enough for one day. I agreed. We turned back to the road and went on. Never did know who he was or where he was going, didn't really want to know."

The Code of the West did not exist separate from the law, and once the law arrived, there had to be lawmen to enforce it. There were two things, aside from honesty and commitment, required to be a good—and I emphasize *good*—law officer "back when." The first was to be better with your gun than anyone else, the second was to be willing to do whatever was required. It helped if those attributes were public knowledge.

James W. Dellinger, Momma's father, was the

police chief in Taylor for more than forty years. He told me that, for the first few years he was an officer, he shot a box of pistol shells just about every day. Once he had gotten good enough, he made a standing offer, at all the turkey shoots in the area, that anyone who wanted to shoot against him, inside pistol range, could use a rifle and he would use a pistol, shooting at any target they chose. Momma said she couldn't remember anyone ever taking him up on his offer in the time she was old enough to pay attention to such things. In the forty-odd years he was police chief, he only drew his pistol once, to knock out a man who had jumped him with a nail-studded club. (The man died a few days later of a brain tumor that had driven him crazy and prompted the attack in the first place.) His reputation with a six-shooter, coupled with his reputation for being fair and color blind, was sufficient to quell almost any problem.

A reputation goes a long way to solving some problems. The Texas Rangers are probably the best known law-enforcement agency in the world. They have been effective largely because people have always known they were effective. As the story goes, there was, back in the last quarter of the nineteenth century, a feud up in North Texas that got a little out of hand. One side had become strong enough to form a mob that was taking over. The city officials, unable to control the situation, wired the state capital for assistance. Word came back from Austin that a Ranger delegation would arrive on the train the next day.

When the train pulled in the next day, the city fathers were waiting at the depot. The mob could be heard, down the street, in the saloon district. Only one man climbed down off the train, a tall man, his face burned a deep tan beneath a broad-brimmed Stetson. A handlebar mustache hid his mouth, but he seemed to be smiling. There was a gunbelt under his coat and a rifle scabbard strapped to his suitcase. He stepped up to the city fathers and identified himself as a Texas Ranger. The city fathers demanded to know where his men were. The Ranger informed them that he didn't have anyone with him.

"But, my God, man, what can one man do?" the city fathers demanded.

The Ranger set down his suitcase, took a cigar out of his coat pocket, and lit it. He blew a cloud of smoke and looked down the street toward the commotion the mob was making. "There isn't but one mob, is there?" he asked.

The story of one Ranger for one mob never happened, but it illustrates a point about the Rangers that anyone who was likely to cross their path had to take into account. And it isn't a made-up point. The Rangers I've met shared that attitude.

When I was working for Game and Fish in Texas, I spent quite a bit of time around Llano County. There was a Ranger stationed at Llano. He was an old man, in the eyes of a twenty-year-old; probably in his sixties. He wore khakis, boots, and a Stetson, but no gunbelt. He carried a .45 automatic tucked down in the waistband of his pants, nestled up against his paunch. He wasn't all that much to look at, until you looked into his eyes. Then you knew that, if the breed ran true, the mob in the previous story would not have had a chance. One of the game wardens, who had known the old Ranger for years, told me this story:

A fellow who lived a few miles outside Llano got into some sort of minor trouble. When a deputy went out to the man's house the next morning to arrest him, he found the place had been turned into a fort. The walls had been reinforced with sandbags, leaving no openings but gun slits at the windows. The man had plenty of ammunition and a good store of food and water; he was ready for a siege. The deputy got behind his car and called for help on his radio. By midafternoon there were more than a dozen lawmen around the house. They had a bullhorn and were trying to talk the man into giving up. The only reply they had gotten thus far was a number of shots that had come dangerously close to the heads of several of the officers. Then the old Ranger arrived.

The Ranger crawled out of his car and took in the men crouched behind cars, trees, and the woodpile. He looked at them, then up at the house, and called to the man who he was and that he was coming up to the house. The man called back that he would shoot anyone who tried to approach him. The old Ranger didn't even draw his pistol; he just walked up the hill to the house, reached through one of the gun slits, and took the man's rifle. He told the man to come on out, and he did. As the other officers ran up the hill, the Ranger walked down, handed the rifle to one of them, got into his car, and drove back to town.

Once they had returned the man to town and gotten him deposited in the jail, one of the deputies asked him why, after he had shot at several of them, he didn't shoot the Ranger when he walked right up to him. The man looked back at the deputy and said, "Didn't you see his eyes? I was scared I wouldn't kill him on the first shot. I knew I wouldn't get a second one."

Police work, like any work, is most successful when knowledge is skillfully applied. I was attending a Christmas party a few years ago, visiting with a gentleman who had spent several years working in the oil patch around Fort Stockton, Texas, when the fields there were first being developed. When he found out D. S. Barker was my great-uncle, he told me this story:

"I was just out of school and had gotten a job surveying sites in the oil patch. I was young, feeling immortal, making good money, and generally full of myself. There were some pretty wild sorts who had come in with the boom. I suppose I was hanging out with some of them part of the time.

"I was walking down the street one morning when I saw Dud Barker on the sidewalk across the street from me. He looked over, recognized me, and crossed the street. We were walking along together, just visiting, when he asked me how I'd slept the night before. I told him I'd slept fine. He said he hadn't, that he'd had a bad dream that had kept him up. He told me he'd dreamed that I was in a poker game with a bunch of hardcases. Then he named not just the men who'd been in the poker game with me the night before, but he described the seating arrangement around the table. He said the dream woke him up and he couldn't go back to sleep for thinking about a poor innocent like me being corrupted by men like that. To this day I don't know how he knew about that game. But there was something in his eyes that told me I was being given one chance and one chance only to clean up my act. I swore off poker playing right then and there."

So it was with the old-time lawmen. Generally, allowing their opponents to know what they could, and would, do, including killing if necessary, prevented many a situation from getting out of hand.

There would have been no need for lawmen in the Old West, or today for that matter, if there were not outlaws. Most outlaws were, as my grandfather referred to them, penny-ante thugs. But there were those few whose names we all know because they passed from reality into legend and became part of the American myth. You recognize the names of the legendary outlaws: Frank and Jesse James, the Youngers, Billy the Kid, Sam Bass, Butch Cassidy and the Sundance Kid, and others.

Why do we still know their names? What were they really like? Why do we remember them when few recall the name of Jim Miller, the most active of the old-time gunfighters? It wasn't because of what they did so much as their personalities—because of what they brought to the job. There is (now don't act surprised) a story that may explain it better than any essay:

John S. Kritzer rode with General Shelby during the Civil War. Frank and Jesse James and Cole Younger had been in Quantrill's Raiders, but they had gotten to know one another when Shelby and Quantrill were involved in joint operations. After the war, the Jameses and Youngers had taken up robbing banks and trains, but Kritzer had gone to Mexico to fight in the revolution there. He had then turned to freighting on the Bozeman Trail and finally gone to Texas and worked for years as a trail driver. He retired in Taylor as an old man and lived peacefully.

After paying their debts to society, Frank James and Cole Younger went on the lecture circuit. (Making a second career out of crime after being caught is nothing new.) On their way to San Antonio to lecture, they had to change trains in Taylor. Knowing that Kritzer lived there, and having time on their hands, they went to visit him. It was right after dinner when the two old outlaws walked up to Kritzer's house. Kritzer was sitting on the front porch, dozing in his rocking chair, when they arrived at his gate. Cole Younger helloed him and Kritzer woke up and peered at him through eyes dimmed with age. Younger laughed and said, "You don't know who I am, do you?" Kritzer, who hadn't seen the two outlaws since the end of the Civil War, forty or fifty years previously, laughed and replied, "Cole Younger, I'd know your ashes in a whirlwind."

I think you'd agree with Kritzer, it's not so much what you do as how you do it. Cole Younger had style. After his capture in Minnesota, when he was

I'd know your ashes in a whirlwind!

139

wounded eleven times, he stood up in the wagon that returned him to town and bowed to the ladies. Such people are remembered, and added to our myths.

Few people remember any specific robberies the Hole-in-the Wall Gang pulled, but we all know of the gang and of its leader, Butch Cassidy. Butch had the style that makes a legendary figure out of a bandit. His style was that of someone who helped his friends, and who considered most people friends. And not just people. I've heard the following story from a couple of folks. I don't know if it really happened, but I do know that in the group photo of the gang, taken in Rawlins, there is a dog in the center of the group.

As I mentioned earlier, the gang took lots of horses along when they left home on their way to pull a job. And the horses had been trained; they were in good shape. But the dog, camp guard and mascot, that went along on at least one trip had not been in training. After they robbed the bank, they left in a bit of a hurry, with a considerable portion of the town's male population in hot pursuit.

The gang members were all well mounted, so, since they knew they would have fresh horses every day, they let their horses out. The posse was pushing, trying to catch up before their horses gave out. The gangs' horses would hold the pace with no trouble, but the dog was another story. He fell behind the gang. They were riding through country studded with boulders when Butch looked back and saw that the posse had finally passed the dog. The trail they were following bent around a rocky hill at that point.

"Boys," Butch called to the gang, "get up in the rocks and play some Winchester music for the locals." The gang pulled up behind the hill, dismounted, and, leaving a couple of men to hold the horses, climbed back up onto the hillside with their rifles. With the first shots, the posse did the sensible thing: they bailed off their horses and took cover behind the rocks. The gang was being careful not to hit anyone, but of course the posse didn't know that, so they stayed under cover, exchanging long-range fire with the gang.

Butch had not dismounted with the rest of the gang, but had continued on around the hill. Staying out of sight, he circled wide around the posse, got behind them and waited. In a few minutes the dog arrived at a slow trot, tongue lolling. Butch took him up on his saddle and circled back slowly, resting his horse. When he got there, the gang fired a final volley, remounted, and headed back up the trail. After a few minutes the posse realized that the gang had fled, and renewed the pursuit, but more cautiously perhaps.

The gang continued to move rapidly the rest of the day. But they took turns carrying the dog. After that, according to one version, the dog was required to train along with the horses. The other man told me that, after that, the gang left the dog at home.

Crime doesn't pay. This is usually taken to mean that the punishment is far worse than any rewards gleaned from the crime—assuming that the criminal is caught. Sometimes though, crime literally doesn't pay, even when that's its goal. I don't know how many stories I've heard of highwaymen waylaying a stage a day early, missing the payroll shipment they had planned on taking. Locked safes have stymied many a bank robber, including, on at least one occasion, the James-Younger gang. Even when everything went according to plan, bank robbers sometimes had to take in extra work. Two men once robbed the bank in Coupland, Texas, and then had to go across the street and hold up the grocery store in order to make a profit for the day.

But of all the ill-fated robberies I've run across, there is one that stands out. One night three men set out to burglarize a bar in Buffalo, Wyoming. It was a simple plan. One man was to hide on the flat, parapeted roof to serve as a lookout while the other two went inside to rifle the cash drawer and safe. The lookout helped force the back door and then, seeing the storeroom piled high with supplies, fortified himself with several bottles before climbing to the roof. The other two men proceeded into the front room of the bar. As they reached the cash register, they looked out of the big plate-glass window right in front of them in time to see two policemen stop to visit on the sidewalk. The burglars ducked behind the bar before the officers saw them. They waited. The cops talked. They waited. The cops still talked. The burglars realized there was plenty of booze around them. They took a drink to settle their nerves. The cops still talked. One drink led to another. The burglars stopped checking, and never noticed that the policemen had left. An hour later the party behind the bar was getting loud enough that one of the cops, returning to the station from his patrol, heard noise in the bar. After calling for help, he entered the bar. He needed help to persuade the burglars that they were indeed under arrest; the drinking had gotten pretty serious by then.

The next morning the lookout awoke with one of the worst headaches you could imagine, trying to figure out what he was doing on the roof of the saloon. The number of empty bottles around him suggested the reason for his headache if not for his location. He half climbed, half fell off the building and went looking for the two friends he vaguely remembered being with the night before. He found them and was invited by the police to join them.

I expect that a hangover as bad as theirs in a setting with as little sympathy as they got would convince most people that, indeed, crime doesn't pay.

As surely as there were lawmen and outlaws, there were lawyers in the West. They have been here since the earliest settlement. My brother, an attorney, pointed out that this section could be very short if I stuck to the old adage, "If you can't say something nice, don't say anything at all." It is true that many people don't like lawyers, but I find them wonderful; they produce a wealth of stories.

A good example of the role of lawyers in a community is the story of a young lawyer who moved into a frontier town and hung out his shingle.

Business was so bad that he wound up having to cowboy to make ends meet. If that doesn't tell you how bad business was, remember that in those days cowboys drew about as poor wages as there were. So no one was particularly surprised to find the young attorney, suitcase in hand, waiting for the stagecoach one day. When someone asked him if he had had enough and was giving up, he replied that he was going back East to recruit another lawyer.

"Another lawyer," his questioner asked, laughing, "what are you going to do with a partner? There isn't enough work for you in this town."

"I didn't say anything about getting a partner. If I can get another lawyer to open an office here, there'll be plenty of work for both of us," was the reply.

It's true, of course. It takes two to make a fight, and in spite of our complaints about them, two lawyers can turn a shooting into a court battle.

The lawless have always liked good lawyers, and our system of honestly attempting to provide justice for all creates some interesting stories. There are stories that are better told without too many specifics about setting, time, and source. Suffice it to say that the following story comes from somewhere along our border with Mexico.

A family living on a little border ranch had struggled for several generations, barely scraping by on scrub cattle and a small freight company that had started with wagons and switched to trucks. Then one year their company received a contract for some deliveries, and they were faced with a problem they hadn't encountered before: they needed to pay taxes. They knew instinctively what Al Capone had to be taught: There are *federales* and then there are *Federales*. You don't mess with the IRS. So they went to a lawyer to get some help with their tax returns, the sort of thing that small-town lawyers do, since there are seldom any full-time accountants around.

"How much did you make last year?" asked the lawyer, who also will remain nameless.

"Well," the patriarch replied, "I've got a few cows and a little trucking company, five trucks. How much should I have made?"

That response was one that would have tipped off a much dumber lawyer than this one to the fact that this was going to be no ordinary tax return. He figured he'd better find out a little more, without finding out too much.

"Did you have any major expenses this year?" he inquired.

The rancher beamed and said, "Yeah, me and my three boys all built our wives new houses. Right out on the place."

"And how much did these houses cost?"

"Well now, I'm not plumb sure what the boys' cost; theirs wasn't nearly as big as mine. Mine was around a couple of hundred thousand."

"And how are you paying for it?"

"Oh, I don't have much to do with banks, I paid cash."

The lawyer said he began to lose interest in how the family was making its money, but figured out that the trucking company probably had a contract that involved pickup and delivery on both sides of the border. He didn't say what he did, but he did point out that everyone is entitled to legal counsel and that that family was certainly in need of it.

Milward Simpson agreed with the lawyer in the last story. Milward was governor of Wyoming and our U.S. senator. Before and after, he was a country lawyer and has always been a great storyteller. He told me once that he felt the obligation to handle cases no matter what he personally thought about the case or the individual. But he added that it was always easier to defend someone you thought had been indicted under a bad law. For instance:

"In 1927, when I was in the Wyoming legislature, there was a bill introduced to create a state law to duplicate the Volstead Act. Some newspaper hung the title 'Still Bill' on it, and as such it went into history.

"I wasn't exactly in favor of the bill or anything else about Prohibition. I once answered a reporter's question about whether I was wet or dry by stating that if I were any wetter I would ripple when the wind blows. But in the case of the Still Bill, I would have opposed it if I had been dry. It was so poorly written that it would make any distillation process illegal. Technically, it made putting a teakettle on the stove illegal.

"So I fought it. And I lost. The bill passed. The day Governor Emerson signed the bill, I mentioned, in front of some reporters, that it was such a bad law that even as poor an old country lawyer as I was could beat it. I went on to say that if I couldn't get someone acquitted who had been indicted under the law, I wouldn't charge a fee.

"The legislative session ended [which didn't take too long, since the Wyoming legislature only meets for forty days—very Biblical—every other year; one of the reasons it's such a good state] and I headed home. Home back then was Thermopolis. When we got off the train, Sharkey Swain, the biggest bootlegger in the Big Horn Basin, was waiting for me. Now Sharkey figured he had an image to maintain. He wore a white linen suit and a long, white silk scarf year around, a real commitment to fashion in that part of the world. He stepped up to me as soon as I was on the depot platform.

"'Milward,' he asked, 'did you mean what you said about the Still Bill?' When I told him that I did, he reached inside his coat and pulled out his indictment. They'd already caught him.

"By the grace of God, a fast outfield, and a good jury, I got Sharkey acquitted. What was interesting was that nothing had been said about what the fee would be if I won, only that it was free if I lost. I just waited to see what Sharkey would do.

"My office was in the old Klink Building, at the head of the stairs on the right. Across the hall was an accountant's office, and behind him, the waiting room for a dentist's office. The dentist's operating room was behind my office. Sharkey came by a week or so after the trial to settle up.

"To understand this, you have to remember that not a single bank failed in Wyoming during the Depression. They had all failed between '25 and '27.

We'd kinda gotten a jump on the Depression, you see. So when Sharkey asked me what he owed me, I told him three hundred fifty dollars, a huge legal fee for that time and place. Sharkey didn't say a word; he just reached into his pocket, pulled out a roll of bills big enough to choke a horse, and started counting out money onto my desk. The roll was mostly ones and fives, but there were plenty of tens and even more than a few twenties.

"The count had gotten up to around two hundred fifty dollars when the dentist, in the room right behind my office, hit a nerve on the woman he had in the chair. She let out a scream like a gut-shot panther. Sharkey never stopped counting, but he looked up and made eye contact with me for the first time.

"That a lawyer back there too?"

One of the rules I've learned about collecting stories is that the kind of people who get into a good deal of trouble may not make the best neighbors, but they are wonderful sources of stories. Laws may not have been thought up for the convenience of storytellers, but the bending, breaking, and enforcing of them has certainly been a great source of material for tellers of tales for time out of mind. And so, I expect, it will continue to be for that much longer.

Lawyers fees

THE GRAND
EXPERIMENT

⋀⋁⋀⋁⋀

By the end of 1918 the
United States had stepped out of our traditional
isolationist position long enough to make the world
safe for democracy. After settling the affairs of the
Old World, we were ready to take on the New. We
turned our back on Europe, with its vast colonial
empires and its constant bickering, and set about
saving ourselves from ourselves. I suppose that saving the world may put you on a moral high horse.
And it seems that high horses are, at times, lofty
enough to put your head in the clouds. However we
mounted it, we were certainly riding one when, with
our collective national eyes at least theoretically
open but clearly unable to see the shape of things to

come, we passed the Volstead Act. Prohibition. It was called the Grand Experiment, and it was: grand in concept, grand in design, grand in effect. The country's saloons, clubs, breweries, distilleries, wineries were closed down. And the people went looking for a drink.

As an experiment, Prohibition illustrated, in huge, sweeping brush strokes, the utter folly of social engineering. Unfortunately, it seems the brush strokes were so huge that someone standing too close could not then, and cannot today, read the message. All moral, philosophical, and legal questions aside, the storytellers of this country should remember to thank Mr. Volstead everyday. He did not save us from ourselves but he did create a wonderfully vibrant piece of American folklore. For if the twenties did indeed roar, the roar was, in part, fueled with bootleg booze. The gangsters that Prohibition produced, or at least catapulted into the realms of folklore, became as important to us as Frank and Jesse James. And Eliot Ness is enshrined next to Wyatt Earp and Pat Garrett.

What most of us know of the history and folklore of Prohibition is largely urban or personal. What has been written or filmed is about the gang wars in Chicago or New York. What most people know of rural stories of Prohibition times are about the Appalachians. In reality, the main impact of Prohition on the stills of the Appalachians was to increase the market. There had been a strong underground whiskey industry there since the federal government passed the whiskey tax in 1792. But, in my travels, largely in the rural parts of the country, I find that everyone who lived through the twenties has stories about Prohibition. Most of them are good.

My grandfather, Pop, was the police chief in Taylor during those years. He corrected me once when I made the statement that you can't legislate morals. "You can legislate them," he pointed out. "You just can't enforce them.

"There was a fellow here that had been struggling along for years with a little bakery. Then, all of a sudden, after Prohibition went into effect, he had money to burn. You didn't have to be a genius to figure out that he had a little business on the side, selling sugar. The Revenue boys used sugar as a way to find bootleggers. It takes a good deal of sugar to keep a still or two going, and the feds would keep track of sugar purchases to locate bootleggers. If you were buying sugar without a good reason, you were likely to get a visit from the feds. Of course a bakery needed sugar, lots of sugar. This old boy had figured that out and was reselling most of what he purchased. I figured that at the height of Prohibition he was using about a ton of sugar to make a dozen doughnuts. But he had a good system. He never was caught.

"Now, here in Williamson County, we split pretty much east and west. The western part of the county, Georgetown and over in there, was dry and over here we were wet. [At that time Taylor was the bigger and richer of the two, located as it was at the junction of two railroads, both with yards and shops there, and surrounded by good farmland; Georgetown was the county seat, though. Things

Sugar
for stills 151

have changed more than a little since then.] Whenever a bootlegger was arrested over here and sent there for trial, the powers that be among the 'wets' made sure that someone who drank got put on the jury. The jury would hang and the bootlegger could stay out, working, until a new trial was called, at which time another 'wet' got on the jury. Their system was a bit awkward, but it worked. Until the time one of the better young whiskey makers in the county was arrested, that is. They got a 'wet' on the jury, of course, and when the jury left for its deliberations, all the spectators adjourned to the café across the street; it takes a jury a long time to admit that it's hopelessly hung. The crowd hadn't even had time to be served, let alone eat, when word came from the courthouse that the jury had returned a guilty verdict. The 'wets' didn't wait for their food, they went hunting their juror with blood in their eyes.

"'Now, boys,' he said when they confronted him, 'stop and think a minute. Ol' Charlie makes fair whiskey, but the best distillers in the state are in Huntsville [the state pen] now. I got the jury to agree to a one-year sentence. Hell, we've just given Charlie a scholarship. When he gets home he'll be making sure-'nough good whiskey.' According to all the reports I heard, such was the case. I suspect that the price rose with the quality, and Charlie was well paid for the time he spent in 'school.'"

During all of Prohibition, Pop, who would, well into his nineties, have an occasional glass of beer or shot of whiskey, never had a drink. He felt that to be a good law officer—he *never* used the word *cop*—he

a good
"law officer"

152

could not be a hypocrite. My other grandfather wasn't a cop, he was just a farmer and a far better than average domino player, which meant, in that part of the world at that time, he was well acquainted with most everyone. It also meant that he was not under the restrictions that Pop was under. He'd been called for jury duty once (in a matter unrelated to Prohibition). He was a good friend of all the officers of the court, since they were all fairly serious domino players. When court recessed at noon, my grandfather met the judge in the hall and was invited to an office in the basement of the courthouse. There they were joined by the prosecuting attorney, the sheriff, and a constable.

"I wasn't at all sure what was going on," my grandfather told Daddy. "The room had a conference table and a pretty good-sized safe in it and nothing else. There was a window, up high in the wall, set at ground level, but it had been painted over. As soon as we were all in the room, the constable closed and locked the door. I was getting more and more curious, since I didn't have a clue as to what was going on. It had all been very quiet, almost formal, as though it was something official and important. Then the sheriff opened the safe and took out a tray with a half-dozen glasses on it. This was followed by another tray with three or four bottles.

'It wouldn't do to have evidence turn up in court that wasn't valid,' the judge told me. 'We always check it to make sure no one has pulled a fast one on us.' [There were many cases during the period of undercover agents buying water or tea, perhaps with enough whiskey spilled on the cork to give the proper smell at time of purchase.]

'We like to get an outside, expert opinion,' the prosecuting attorney added.

"I did my duty as a citizen," my grandfather concluded to Daddy, slowly and carefully. "I never knew who had made that whiskey, but I always wished him well."

There was a family living up the creek from my folks who supplemented the income of their little place by working as a haying crew. As the boys grew up, they went into the business in a big way for that part of the world. There were three grown boys and their father. Aside from learning the haying business, the boys had learned an overappreciation of the bottle from their daddy. Along toward the end of Prohibition they had acquired a new baler and a tractor to pull it. One day they were working in a little hayfield behind my folks' house. One of the boys had been lucky and found someone with whiskey to sell that morning, so, when they broke at noon, they retired to the shade and drank their lunch. Mother said she was working in the kitchen when they came back to work. She could hear them trying to start the tractor without much luck. She was not paying close attention to them, but did hear one of them ask if it had gas in it. Another, his speech slightly slurred, volunteered to check. Mother said the next thing she heard was a big bang. She headed for the back door at a run to go see what had happened. As she came outside, she saw a hat floating down from the sky and Daddy laughing.

"What are they doing?" Momma called.

"Sobering up," Daddy responded.

Tractors were still new then, and people were learning how they worked. The idea that using the light of a match to see if there was any fuel in the gas tank had seemed like a good one, at least to a group of men who had been fueling their own gas tanks just minutes before. Fortunately, the tractor was out of gas and the haying crew came out of the explosion with nothing more than some missing eyebrows and, uncharacteristically, the ability to drive the tractor in a straight line that afternoon.

Those fellows would drink just about anything that would pour out of a bottle, but for most people who wanted a drink during Prohibition there was the search not just for alcohol, but for potable alcohol.

Mendel Booth, the banker in Taylor who bought the town's first car, wasn't averse to taking a drink, a pleasure he did not deny himself just because of Mr. Volstead. By the time Prohibition was wearing on toward its end, Mendel was no longer a young man. He attended a bankers' convention in San Antonio during a period when there had been a rash of poisoning from jackleg whiskey. (Jackleg whiskey was the name given to the sort of improperly distilled whiskey that could seriously injure or even kill the drinker. Blindness was one of the most common reactions to jackleg.) One night Mendel sat in on a poker game in one of the hotel rooms at the convention. Mendel was old and used to an early bedtime.

The hour, coupled with the bottle that passed around the table, made Mendel drowsy. He would bet, doze off, have to be awakened, and have the play reviewed so he could bet again. The other players, all friends of Mendel, became tired of the routine. The conversation turned to the subject of jackleg whiskey and its effects. The other players made sure Mendel got the message, in his waking moments, then opened a fresh bottle and mentioned they weren't too sure of the reliability of the source. The bottle made a round, and play continued. Mendel dozed off within a minute or two. They waited until Mendel started snoring, pulled the curtains, turned off the lights, then woke Mendel and talked as though the game were going on normally. Mendel awoke, looked at his cards and saw nothing, total blackness. At that point Mendel inadvertently turned the tables (and the table) on his tormentors. He jumped up and tipped the table over. Cards, chips, money, whiskey, and glasses flew everywhere in the darkness as Mendel screamed, "Oh my God, I've gone blind!"

The search for potable drink took many forms. Uncle Emzy gave Josh a bottle once. Seeing him a week or so later, he asked how the whiskey had been. "Jest right," Josh replied. "What do you mean by 'just right'?" Uncle Emzy asked. "Well, Mr. Emzy," Josh replied, "if it'd been any better, you'd have kept it, and if it'd been any worse, I couldn't have drunk it." There were others who faced a real problem, the winos. No provisions were made in the Volstead Act for the seriously addicted. Those whose addictions were serious enough to prevent their holding decent jobs were faced with a crisis, one often met with creativity if not good judgment. Sterno, filtered through bread, yielded a theoretically drinkable alcohol, though Pop told me he had seen men killed, blinded, or left spastic from it.

Most people in need of a drink weren't as desperate as the winos but they could be even more creative. For instance, vanilla extract sales skyrocketed during Prohibition. Since vanilla extract is used in small doses in cooking, and since the heat of cooking evaporates the alcohol, many people don't realize that it runs seventy proof. There were tough old tobacco-chewing coots, most of whom had never even seen a toothbrush, who, for the duration of Prohibition, had as sweet a breath as anyone could ask for. By a similar set of circumstances, there were a number of patent medicines that gained in popularity during the period. Some of these, whose restorative powers were open to more question than most, were forced from the market. Others survived scrutiny and did a brisk business. But perhaps the story that best illustrates the medicinal use of whiskey during the period is a story of its use as a snakebite remedy. I've heard variations of the story throughout the West and the South; I expect it was told wherever there were poisonous snakes. The way I first heard it, the fellow who told it one morning over coffee said:

"Ol' Warren lived out in the breaks along the Frio. That's about as snaky a piece of country as you'll run into anywhere. There were several denning sites on his place, so, spring and fall, he was pretty well over-run with 'em. Well, my point is that it took some-thing special in the line of rattlesnakes to impress ol' Warren. So the day he brings one into town to show off, it draws a crowd. There's not much happening in town that week, so the newspaper editor sends somebody down to talk to Warren and write up a lit-tle piece about the monster snake he's killed. Fred, down at the Feed and Seed, was the town photogra-pher back then, had pictures of everything that hap-pened hanging all over his office. So he brings his camera to get a picture of this big rattler.

"Ol' Warren's only about five foot six, so he's got his arm up high over his head to stretch the snake out good. He's holding it by the tail, shaking it some so it rattles a little. All of a sudden, ol' Warren notices that he ain't the only one shaking the snake's tail. He looks down and realizes that just hitting a snake that size over the head may have not been the best plan for killing it, even if you were planning to skin it and have the hide mounted. The snake is clearly not dead; it is coming to, probably with a bad headache, and is somewhat upset with ol' Warren. He drops it like it was a live rattlesnake, but he's too slow. It's already reached up and nipped him just above the top of his boot.

"Feed and Seed was the kind of place that at-tracted all kinds of critters, some to eat the feeds and seeds and some to eat what ate the feeds and seeds. Anyway, Fred had all kinds of traps and cages, so when ol' Warren started screaming about not killing the snake—I kinda think he may have been making plans to do that himself—Fred brought a cage, and several of the men herded the creature into it. Doc was out on one of the ranches delivering a baby, so they packed ol' Warren into the drugstore to see if Old Man MacCallen, the druggist, could do anything for him. MacCallen knew all the accepted treatments of the day. He put a tourniquet on ol' Warren's leg, cut incisions over the fang marks, and let the poison drain out. Once ol' Warren had quieted down and was resting peacefully, Old Man MacCallen went into the back of the drugstore and came back with a bottle of pure grain alcohol and gave ol' Warren a stiff drink. The spectators lost interest in ol' Warren's recovery and started licking suddenly parched lips, wondering at the sight of a bottle of legal medicinal alcohol.

"I was at the sale barn that day. I'd brought in a bunch of dry cows, since the market had picked up some with the greening grass. When word reached the sale barn about ol' Warren getting snakebit and being up at the drugstore, I headed up there to see how he was doing. I'as scared. I'd know ol' Warren since I'as no more than a pup, when Daddy would send me over to ride for him to help gather those rough breaks pastures of his. Whatever kind of hand I made was because of what he'd taught me of catching wild cows in rough country. I didn't want to see him die of snakebite. Truth is, that wasn't the first time, or the last, ol' Warren got snakebit. Living where he did, it just happened sometimes. I suspect he probably was pretty nearly immune to them by then, because by the time I finally got to the drugstore, he seemed in good spirits and the leg was hardly swollen at all. It had taken me a while to get to the drugstore, though. Word of the accident and the treatment, with particular emphasis placed on the big shot of pure grain alcohol—legal, medicinal, pure grain alcohol—had spread around town like a fire on a dry, windy day. I didn't drink back then— still don't—so I hadn't realized how hard it had become to get a drink around here. By the time I got to the drugstore, there was a line from there down to the end of the block and around the corner. Men were waiting for the snake to rest up and produce more venom."

For people living on the border with either Mexico or Canada, Prohibition did not, for most of its time, impose much of a hardship. All you had to do was cross the border and you could enjoy the pleasures of a legal saloon or wine with your supper. And if you were reasonably careful, you could cross back over the border with a pint bottle in your boot that no one would notice. Crossing with larger quantities was both much more profitable and much more dangerous. The porosity of the border varied from place to place and time to time. Uncle Dud stopped many a mule train crossing the Rio Grande into Pecos County while he was sheriff. Uncle Dud was not opposed to drinking, would take a drink himself, but didn't drink during Prohibition and didn't allow drinking in Pecos County. (He didn't even cross the river to drink in Mexico, since he wasn't allowed to carry a gun into Mexico and there were people down

there who would have liked to catch him without a
six-shooter.) He dried the county up enough to
prompt the following literary effort to appear, anony-
mously, in a local newspaper:

I am way out in western Texas
Where the Pecos waters flow,
Just across the bridge from Stockton,
But it's there I long to go.

I have gone by Buena Vista,
And I have tried the Sheffield road,
But old D.B. was there waiting,
And he captured all our load.

If I could get my goods to Stockton,
To those boys whose throats are dry,
I could soon command a fortune,
But D.B. won't let me by.

I have whiskey, beer and brandy,
And I could take a little jake,
But that doesn't make no difference,
For all but the label is a fake.

I am anchored here at Crossett,
With McCamey by my side,
But there is so much competition,
That it makes us peddlers ride.

* * *

But it isn't long 'til election,
Then if D.B.'s on the job,
I am going to hunt new country,
And sell that Territory to Bob.

For perhaps he doesn't know him,
And will try to make it thru,
But alas I see his finish,
Over in that Stockton Zoo.

Pecos County territory for sale, cheap
  See Secretary, Bootleggers' Association

The coasts provided quite a few entry points into the country without benefit of customs agents. In 1980 I spent some time on Ossabaw Island, near the mouth of the Savannah River in Georgia. Queenie Mae Williams worked on the island, had for years, but back in the twenties she had been a torch singer on the Southern black nightclub circuit. When times got hard in the early thirties, Queenie Mae had supported her family with a little business she ran upstairs. She lived in an old house in Savannah that had been converted into two apartments, one upstairs and one downstairs. She lived downstairs and rented the upstairs flat in the name of a man who actually resided in the cemetery across the street. He paid his rent in cash, by mail. His flat contained a still that produced a heady product referred to as Scrap Iron. The place was never raided, but if it had been, there was no way to trace the still to Queenie. When I knew her, fifty years later, Queenie still made excellent dandelion wine, occasionally cut with Scrap Iron, all strictly for personal consumption. Queenie was retired and had become an excellent singer of gospel music and spirituals, but on occasion she required a tonic for her blood.

I was walking along the causeway with Queenie one evening, watching the sunset. During supper I had seen a shrimp boat slip into Ossabaw Sound and anchor. This was not an unusual occurrence. Shrimpers, wanting a good night's sleep but not wanting to go all the way up the river to Savannah, would often anchor in the quiet water of the sound and return to fishing early the next morning. As Queenie and I walked along in the twilight, I heard a fast power boat screaming down the river. In a few minutes it had crossed the sound and pulled up next to the shrimp boat. It was tied to the shrimper for no more than two minutes, probably less, then cut loose and headed, again at high speed, back up the river toward Savannah.

"What do you reckon they were doing?" I asked Queenie.

"Same thing they would have been doing fifty, sixty years ago. Some things don't change," she replied.

Distance from the border was a deciding factor in what you drank during Prohibition. Along the borders, smuggling was safer than running stills, plus the fact that bonded liquors commanded a higher price, since the quality was guaranteed (assuming that someone wasn't reusing bottles and counterfeiting seals). But there was a distance beyond which it was cheaper and safer to make booze than to smuggle it in. The distance varied depending on the roads and the market, but southern Montana or northern Wyoming was about the break point for whiskey coming in from Canada. Occasionally, bonded Canadian whiskey showed up, but mostly it was homemade.

Curly Witzel told me that he had managed to get out of Sheridan once with a pint of good Canadian whiskey in his saddle pocket. "I'as horseback," he told me, "headed back out to Eatons' at a leisurely pace, when I met a couple of friends, or so I'd thought up until then, who were riding for the PK, out hunting strays. Neither of them had been to town for quite a spell—had been up on the mountain for most of the summer, in fact. We pulled up in some shade along the creek, got down to visit, loosened our cinches, and let our horses graze. We talked about the weather [which, I might remind you, is not idle gossip in cow country], the grass, what I'd heard of calf prices in town, whether I'd cut sign of any wandering cattle, and then settled in to gossiping. When we figured our horses had rested enough, we caught 'em, pulled our cinches, and mounted.

"'Say,' Bobby asked me, 'you didn't get out of town with a bottle, did you?'

"I hadn't really planned on mentioning that pint bottle to anyone. I hadn't had any bonded whiskey in quite a while, and I figured to sorta save that for myself. But they were friends, and besides I might be thirsty someday when one of them was coming from town. So I reached into my saddle pocket and pulled the bottle out. It suddenly looked awfully small, but I passed it to them. Bobby broke the seal, opened it, and took a polite swig before passing it on to Fred.

"Fred wasn't old enough to have frequented saloons before Prohibition. He was used to drinking whatever was available. He was partial enough to booze that before Prohibition was over he developed a callus on the bridge of his nose from the rims of Mason jars resting on it so much. He eyed that little bottle, put it to his lips, tilted his head back, and opened his throat. When he'd finished, he carefully screwed the cap back on the empty bottle and returned it to me, saying, 'You know what, Curly, that's good whiskey. Somebody could make some real money off that stuff.' I didn't feel like that was the time to explain to him that the Seagram's company had done all right for some little time selling that stuff."

In Sheridan, you generally didn't have to worry about all the quality of booze; there were good, reputable bootleggers. I have probably heard as many bootlegging stories from Sam Mavrakis as I have from anyone. And Sam knows whereof he speaks: his daddy did as much or more than anyone to ensure that Sheridan County was not unduly inconvenienced by the Volstead Act.

Harry Mavrakis came to Sheridan from Greece to work in the coal mines that were the center of the economy for the area. He was injured in the mines, and the company set him up as operator of the pool hall in the company town next to the mine. The pool hall sold refreshments and had a couple of poker tables in the back. It was a good business, and he was a good businessman; within a few years he was able to open his first business in Sheridan, the Bronc Pool Hall. He continued to prosper and opened a second business, the Ritz, a café, pool hall, and gambling parlor. When Prohibition arrived, Harry found he had another talent that was suddenly in demand; he knew how to make beer, wine, and whiskey. And, as I have been assured by a number of people who sampled it and can tell the difference between good and bad booze, it was all good.

"Daddy would get arrested," Sam told me, "and sentenced to jail for a month or so. But he only had to be there at night. They let him out during the day so he could support his family. And so no one in town got thirsty. He would leave jail and go directly to his still to work, returning to the jail every night to sleep. My brothers and I were on the high school football team then. One time we got our names in the paper the same time Daddy got arrested. Now he never did learn to read English, but somebody showed him the paper that day and that night, at supper, he pulled it out, laughing, and told us we weren't as good as he was; our names were on page four but his was on page one.

"Another thing about those days. Around here, at least, there weren't the problems you read about in other places. I guess in the cities there were problems. I guess in the cities there were fights about who controlled bootlegging, but we all had the attitude that there was plenty of work for everyone. Why, if someone was short on supplies, or even booze, one of the other bootleggers would lend him what he needed. We all got along fine."

Sheridan was like most small towns in the rural West. Mr. Volstead simply put a new set of conventions in place; he didn't really change the basic pattern of life. One of the special changes that did occur in the mountains of the West, Bill Daniels told me about. The Forest Service was beginning to work seriously at saving the national forests from fires. In some areas Mr. Volstead made it necessary for fire lookouts to learn a new code of conduct. Whiskey Mountain may have been named for a still placed on it by fur traders in the nineteenth century, but it lived up to its name during Prohibition. There were a number of "factories" working there during those days. The problem was that the stills would produce, on occasion, wisps of smoke that looked amazingly like the wisps of smoke produced by the early stages of a forest fire, during which a fire crew had some hope of putting the fire out. "You can imagine," Bill said, "how you would feel if a fire crew showed up at your still. Don't get me wrong; there wouldn't be any repercussions with the law. They'd mostly be friends who had just hiked a long way because you couldn't build a fire that didn't smoke. They would probably feel uncommonly thirsty and could easily drink up two or three days' profits, since you couldn't really expect them to pay, after you had made them hike all that way for nothing. The trick was to make sure the lookouts were people you could trust. Then all that was required was for someone to point out to them where smoke did not mean fire. Amazingly enough, we had almost no trouble during the whole period." Probably in part, I suspect, because places like Dubois had about the same priority as the far side of the moon for the feds.

Rural areas are often overlooked by government because there aren't enough people in rural areas to figure into the maximum-good-for-the-maximum-number equation. That was the case for the federal revenue agents during Prohibition, with a few exceptions. There were rural areas, though, that were close enough to cities to become major "manufacturing" centers. These areas attracted the attention of the feds. There were some parts of Deep East Texas that were supplying not only their own neighbors but Houston, Dallas, and New Orleans; the feds decided to take a closer look. Virgil Dupree was working for the government back in those days, and wound up in East Texas. Mr. Dupree used to take me hunting with him when I was in high school. As we drove through some wooded country on our way to his deer lease one year, we saw a thin wisp of smoke rising above the trees. It stopped and I commented that the fire must have gone out.

"Not necessarily," he replied. "There was a time when I'd have felt obligated to check out a little plume of smoke like that one. The old boys who ran the stills over in East Texas could build a fire that wouldn't smoke at all—except sometimes, when they first started them, they wouldn't draw right until they built up a bit of heat. If you were out looking and got lucky, what you saw was just about like that." I, of course, started quizzing him about the time and place. This, among all the facts and background, is what he told me:

"Now, this story is probably apocryphal," he said, "but it sums up how things were in that part of the world back then. [I hadn't encountered *apocryphal* before, but after I got home and looked it up, I hung on to it as a very useful word for a collector and teller of tales.] I worked in the office more than in the field; accountants were not as glamorous as the field men, but they caught more bootleggers. The field men had all the good stories, though." One day George Fielder, one of the field men, had come into their office looking pale and drawn. When Mr. Dupree questioned him, he told this story.

"I went out in the tulies to check out a fellow we'd gotten a tip about. His place was at the end of a very bad road, way back in the swamp. When I got there, there wasn't anyone at the old ramshackle house but a kid about five or six years old. I asked him where his daddy was.

"'Pappy's at the still,' he replied, big as life, and I started getting interested; figured maybe I wasn't on a wild-goose chase after all. I asked about his mother and got the same response. When I asked about older brothers and sisters, I discovered that everyone in the family except this kid was working at the still. I knew I'd hit pay dirt: I'd found a kid who wasn't old enough to know to keep his mouth shut around strangers. I had visions of catching the whole family red-handed, so I told the kid I'd give him two bits to take me to the still.

"'Give me the money,' the kid said, real quick. And I knew I had the whole family as good as caught. I told the kid I'd give him the money when we got back.

"'You better give me the money now, mister,' the kid said. 'You ain't coming back.'"

Mr. Dupree said that Fielder didn't think they had enough men to go back into that swamp. He figured the family continued to make whiskey until Prohibition ended.

Prohibition was, from the start, an idea whose time may have come politically, but it had not come culturally. Virtually no one who wanted a drink had to do without. Yet, given human and political nature, once the Grand Experiment was started, it was hard to stop. Through the Roaring Twenties we drank to celebrate the good times. Beginning in '29, we drank to drown our sorrows. But, though the law was roundly ignored, it continued in effect into FDR's first term. Roosevelt wanted to do away with the Volstead Act for two reasons: first, he figured the country could, collectively, use a drink; second, he figured the government could use all the tax money that the country currently wasn't paying for each bottle it drank. There was no single thing that brought the supporters of Mr. Volstead to give up (many of them never did); it was the total of all the evidence that finally caused most of them to accept the fact that the Experiment wasn't working, and probably never had. One of my favorite stories of how one of the supporters finally came around may not be factual, but it certainly is true. I heard it from Uncle James, who, claiming Lyndon Johnson as his source, told it this way:

"Back in those days, the White House staff was considerably smaller than it is today, and the house staff had Sunday evenings off. FDR, Eleanor, various of the cabinet members, advisers, Secret Service men, and supper guests would simply raid the icebox. They'd make a meal of heated-up leftovers or sandwiches. It was an informal time, and Roosevelt excelled at using such homey settings to push points he was trying to make with cabinet members or invited congressmen.

"One night the President had invited a congressman who was parchedly dry and seemed determined not only to stay that way himself but to keep the country, at least legally, in the same condition. Roosevelt, desperate to find some tax money to help finance his schemes for fighting the Depression, was twisting the congressman's arm. The President had been arguing the issue from a practical, pragmatic point of view, the congressman from a moral one. The discussion had lasted for some little time when they adjourned to the kitchen to fix supper. Sandwiches in hand, they were sitting down when Roosevelt, returning to the discussion, said, 'Well, what about beer, then?' Before the congressman could reply, a Secret Service man who was preparing to sit at the table said, 'Yes sir,' and left the room.

"Twenty minutes later, while the President and the

congressman were still wrangling over the repeal of
Prohibition, the Secret Service man returned with a
case of beer. The congressman was aghast until he
realized that Roosevelt's question to him about legal-
izing beer had been misunderstood by the Secret
Service man as a request for a beverage to go with a
sandwich. If a Secret Service agent could buy beer
that easily, that close to the White House, the congressman allowed, the law clearly wasn't working
and maybe they needed to look at it a little closer.
When he stopped fighting the repeal at every turn, it
really began to pick up speed in Congress. It wasn't
too long before we could drink in public again."

Prohibition was a moral issue, and the people who
really believed that over time we would be better for
it didn't give up easily. The result was that the repeal
wasn't as simple as the passage. The repeal became a
states' rights issue. Each state, often each county or
even each precinct, got to vote on how it would handle liquor. The term "local option" took on a special
meaning, especially through the Bible Belt. The center line of Main Street in Bartlett, Texas, follows the
county line between Williamson and Bell counties.
Williamson County voted wet while Bell voted dry in
the local-option elections. The Depression had left
more than a few buildings in Bartlett vacant. As the
economy picked up again, buildings on the south side
of Main Street opened first, with bars that couldn't
locate in cheaper buildings across the street.

There were places where local-option elections
were so close that recounts and lawsuits resulted. In

other places the results of the vote were a formality, a formality that suggested a party might be in order. Such was the case in Gillespie County, Texas. Prince Carl of Solms-Braunfels and Otfried Hans Freiherr von Meusebach, known locally as John O. Meusebach, relocated several thousand Germans to Texas in the 1840s and located them on lands in the limestone hills of the Edwards Plateau. They made a successful treaty with the Comanches and started farming and running cattle. Ninety years later their descendants were still there. If you wanted to pick a single word to describe the area, it would be *solid*. Solid people of solid beliefs, living in solid stone houses set on solid farms, as little affected by the Depression as any farming area could be. The older generations still were very German, many people speaking little if any English. Prohibition had been a bit of a mystery to many of them, and a mighty inconvenience; they liked to visit with friends while they had a beer or two.

When the Volstead Act was repealed, it took the citizens of Gillespie County little time to schedule their local-option election. When the polls closed that evening in Fredericksburg, the county seat, the ballot boxes were brought out onto the front steps of the courthouse and opened. Ballots were removed one at a time and read aloud to the waiting crowd, a crowd that included almost everyone in the county because the bars along Main Street were prepared to open their front doors for the first time in years. The citizens of Gillespie County were ready to put Mr. Volstead behind them. The head of the county commission, an older, highly respected gentleman to whom English was a second language, read the ballots in a booming voice that carried across the courthouse lawn:

"Vet...vet...vet...vet...drrry...vet...vet..." on and on for several minutes, until, "Vet...vet...drr—why, that son of bitch voted twice!" Supporters of Mr. Volstead were not plentiful in Gillespie County.

GHOST STORIES

ΛΛΛΛΛ

Every storyteller knows
some ghost stories. Generally we save them for dark
nights with low, flickering light. Under the right conditions, ghost stories allow a teller to give his audience what is best described as a delightful scare. At
other times we try to leave the sense of just possible
mystery. Generally, though, we listen to them with
salt shaker in hand, much more ready to be teased
than to believe. My attitude about ghost stories
changed while I was working for the Triangle X
Ranch in the summer of 1969.

That summer I spent as much time as I could visiting with Harold Mappes. He was a gentleman in
his eighties, called Skipper since, among his many

occupations, he had been a sailor and an officer in the merchant marine. I was sharing a room in the main house with Bill Manning, across the hall from Skipper's room. One Saturday night, Bill had gone to town while I stayed at the ranch to listen to some of Skipper's stories.

We went to bed around nine-thirty or ten, and I slept well until around midnight. I awoke then to the realization that it was not Bill, or anyone else I knew, who had come into the room through the closed window across the room from the door. I was, very suddenly, wide awake and aware that he wasn't someone so much as he had been someone, or someone had been him, or maybe he still was someone. I've never been clear on tenses when referring to ghosts. I've also never known how to address a stranger in my room, a person or a ghost, who has a scar from ear to ear, under his chin, around his throat. He'd either been hanged or had his throat cut, unsuccessfully. It was clearly a scar and not a wound; whatever had made it hadn't killed him.

There was a distinct chill in the air as he stood there, looking at me. I felt fear, surprise, awe, all of the reactions appropriate to seeing a ghost. But there was something in his face that made me realize he wasn't there for me. He moved across the room and through the door, which impressed me because he didn't bother to open it. I knew he was looking for Skipper. Skipper had worked in the gold mines around Cananea in Sonora, Mexico, around the turn of the century. He'd been there during the

"Yaqui Revolt," and had told me several stories and shown me photos of that part of his life. It dawned on me, as I leaped from bed and headed for the door, behind the ghost, that he was dressed like the Yaquis I'd seen in Skipper's photos. He must have been either a comrade or an enemy of Skipper's. I jerked the door open. The hall was empty, so I crossed to Skipper's room. I stopped with my hand on the doorknob, though. I could see that this was not my affair, and that my intruding would probably cause more harm than good. I went back to bed. I did not, however, go back to sleep. Bill came in an hour or so later, and we talked for a while before he went to sleep. I said nothing to Bill, and spent most of the rest of the night listening to Bill snore and waiting for something to happen across the hall. Nothing did.

The next morning at breakfast I was a bit worse for wear, not having had a great deal of sleep. When Skipper came down, I asked him how his night had been. Something must have shown on my face, because he looked at me closely before responding with a simple "Good." My look asked for more. He smiled the smile of an old man who had seen more than I was ever likely to, and said, "Nothing happened that I couldn't handle." There the subject ended. I never found out who the Yaqui was, how he got the scar, or what he and Skipper had to talk about. I never saw him again, so I hope—knowing Skipper, I *expect*—that whatever brought him there was resolved. All I know is that I lost a good night's sleep, and apparently Skipper didn't. I've always enjoyed ghost stories, and since that night I've never dismissed one out of hand.

The Yaqui ghost had traveled over a thousand miles to see Skipper. I don't know whether that's a long, hard journey for a ghost. I do know that ghosts are often associated with a particular place. Manuel Valdez told me such a story.

Manuel was born and reared on a big ranch under the Sleeping Lady, a mountain across the Rio Grande from Del Rio. Manuel was not a violent man, and the chaos and violence of the revolution didn't sit well with his quiet love of animals and people, so along about 1915, he crossed the River. For years he worked as a cowboy and sheepherder in the San Angelo area before coming to work for Daddy. Manuel had lived a long life by then, a life of comfortable solitude. He was an old man with shoulder-length white hair and long beard. He could go long periods without talking, but he had a treasure trove of folk and natural-history lore. He was an excellent horseman and storyteller, which means that I spent as much time with him as I could, growing up.

One evening, after we'd tended to chores, we sat watching the sunset and visiting. I don't remember how the subject of ghosts came up but, when it did, he told me this story.

In the old days, some time after Juarez and before Villa, there were times of anarchy in parts of northern Mexico. During one of those times a bandit gang was started by a singular captain. He was a tall, angular man whose dark eyes, high cheekbones, and aquiline nose spoke of Spanish and Indian ancestry. The gang's success indicated his intelligence, and the scar from jaw to hairline across his left cheek hinted at his ruthlessness.

When the gang had accumulated more wealth than could safely be distributed and handled, the captain would take two men to help handle the pack mules, retire to the mountains, and hide the loot. The two men were then handsomely paid and sent north of the River. That was the story the captain told when he returned alone from each trip.

Ramón Chavez and his best friend had joined the gang as youths to escape their lives of poverty. After five years of raiding, battles, and camp life, they had had their fill of the bandit life. When the captain chose them to accompany him to hide a portion of treasure, they were ready and willing to leave the outlaw trail. Still, they wondered whether the captain paid in gold or lead. They proceeded cautiously.

Heavily loaded mules travel slowly. A full week passed before they reached their goal. They filled all their water bottles and goatskin bags one morning before the captain led them over a pass into a small valley. There had been a spring feeding a small creek at one time, but it had dried, and the trees around it and along the streambed struggled to survive. A stone cabin stood beside the spring, but its inhabitants were not rooted there as the trees were. Its windows and door were black holes, the wooden frames faded to the color of the stone walls. The trail was as faded as the wood. Few had seen this valley, this cabin, in years.

They camped at the cabin that night. The captain said he had strong connections to the cabin, but would say nothing of what they were. Early the next morning they climbed the steep slope above the cabin. Three-quarters of the way up, hidden by a wing of rock, was a cave. Inside, mounds not unlike graves littered the floor and caused Ramón and his friend to look back at the captain. He seemed not to notice their looks, or their hands sliding to their pistols. He simply brought in the picks and began to bring in the panniers containing the bags of treasure.

They buried all but four bags of the treasure. The captain gave each man a packhorse to carry his wealth as well as his food and water. While Ramón and his friend packed, the captain went into the cabin. For several minutes they could hear him singing and chanting, his voice too low to understand. He came out as they finished packing and told them he would show them the fork in the trail so they could go to Texas while he returned to the gang.

It was a spring day, drawing to summer, thunderheads in the mountains producing rains that had the rivers running big and muddy. The trail crept up the side of a mountain and wound along the edge of a canyon wall. The thunderheads had dumped their rains upstream the night before, and the stream, a hundred feet below, ran high and red with the runoff of many side canyons.

Ramón was in front, leading a pack mule. The beauty of the day and the load on his mule caused his mind to wander. He was thinking of the little rancho he would buy when he heard a pistol cock. He twisted to his right, over the cliff edge, and was reaching for his pistol when the first shot rang out and his friend fell from his saddle. Ramón got his pistol out, but was looking into the deep black eyes of the captain, over his gun barrel. Ramón ducked as the captain fired, and the bullet clipped his jacket at the shoulder. He lost his balance and pitched over the cliff.

He hit the river on his back, knocking the wind out of himself, and almost inhaled a lungful of water before he fought back to the surface. For the next couple of miles he was only concerned with trying to keep his head above water. When he finally crawled onto a sandbar, he was more dead than alive. As he lay there trying to recover his strength, his friend and the horses and mules, stripped of their loads, drifted by. For two days Ramón hid in the brush along the canyon floor, until he was sure the captain believed him dead. Then he headed north.

A month later Ramón stood on the south bank of the Rio Bravo, footsore, hungry, and owning only the ragged clothes he wore. But, halfway across, the river would become the Rio Grande and he would be in Texas, and safe. He found work, first as a sheepherder and then as a cowboy. He swore off the tequila he'd loved as a youth, and saved his money. Within fifteen years of crossing the river, Ramón had saved enough to marry and to buy a small place of his own.

The little rancho was not as large as the one Ramón had dreamed of that distant day on the canyon rim. But it was home, a nice adobe house with an arbor to add to the shade of a lone mesquite tree. There was a large garden and a little flock of goats for food. Ramón could get work as needed to provide the little money he and his wife needed. It was a comfortable enough life, and Ramón never talked of and seldom even thought of his past in Mexico. But stories travel, slowly at times, but they travel.

Twenty years after Ramón had stood on the south bank of the River, half starved and owning nothing, he found himself on the north bank, looking south. Now he was, if not wealthy, at least no longer poor. He and his wife were in a new, large wagon. Their supplies took up little space in the wagon. Ramón figured to have the wagon filled with more important things. The story that had brought them here was an old one, told by a one-legged sheep shearer from near Ramón's old home in Mexico. The story was of how he had lost his leg.

He was a young man, full of fire and hungry for adventure when he had joined the *rurales* to fight Indians and bandits. His zest was in no way diminished by several fights with the Apaches and one or two brushes with a large gang of bandits. His last fight, the sheepshearer said, was a real battle with a gang of bandits. The *rurales* had information that the gang would attack the mule train loaded with bullion while it camped at a remote water hole. They ambushed the gang there and killed them all.

The leader of the gang fought like a wild man, killed several troopers, and would have escaped except that the storyteller barred his path. "I had to step clear of the boulder I hid behind to get a good shot," he said. "We shot at the same moment, or perhaps I shot a fraction of a second sooner and my bullet ruined his aim. For my shot punctured his heart, stone though it was, while his shattered my knee." In such a remote place there was no medical help. The leg had to be amputated.

Ramón had questioned the sheepshearer at length about where and when the battle took place. Ramón had him describe the man who had shot him. It was Ramón's old captain. He had died less than a year after Ramón's escape into Texas. Ramón was the only man alive who knew where the bandits' treasure was hidden. There was limitless wealth waiting for him to claim it.

Two months passed before they rolled the wagon over the faint trail into the little valley where the cabin stood watch below the hidden cave. The stream was still dry, the trees and brush still struggling to survive. The cabin stood, its roof sagging and its windows and door dark shadows in the light stone walls. They camped in the scant shade of the trees next to the dry stream, two hundred sun-baked yards from the cabin. The next morning his wife stayed in camp while Ramón went up the slope behind the cabin.

Ramón found the cave exactly where he remembered it, behind the wing of rock. Inside, the mounds littered the floor just as he remembered them. But he dug all day and found nothing. He knew how deep they had buried the gold, and dug twice that deep. Nothing. He dug in other mounds. Nothing.

He dug between mounds. The same. He worked all day, but when he came out into the late-afternoon sun, he had nothing to show for it but sweat.

When he reached the campsite, his wife tried to console him. She said he must have found the wrong cave. What better way to hide a cave than to have it in a place where there were other similar caves? Ramón decided to go back and scout around the hill-side. After he had something to eat. While she was feeding Ramón, his wife told him that she was short of cornmeal and wondered if the people in the cabin might let them have some.

Ramón told her that no one had lived there for more than twenty years. He pointed out that the door was missing and the roof was ready to collapse. But she insisted that the man who lived there had stopped and visited with her shortly before Ramón returned. He had tied his horse behind the cabin and gone in. Certainly, she told him, if Ramón hadn't seen the man, he must have heard him singing that strange song as he came down the hill and past the cabin.

The hair stood up on the back of Ramón's neck as he retrieved his six-shooter from the wagon and walked over to the cabin. There was no horse tied behind the cabin, and there were no tracks anywhere around the place, not even any mice or insect tracks in the dust of the cabin floor.

Ramón demanded that his wife describe her visitor.

"He was tall, aloof, proud. His eyes were dark, almost black, and very deep. He was handsome, even with the scar on his cheek."

"The scar," Ramón demanded, "was it thus?" He

indicated a long scar from hairline to jaw on his left cheek. "And he rode a horse, black with a white star? With a silver-trimmed saddle?"

"Yes," she said. "You did see him, then?"

"Not for twenty years," Ramón replied, returning to their camp and beginning to pack. It was late, but he had no intention of spending the night in the same valley with the ghost of his captain.

As an old man, Ramón reflected that he was just as well off. If he had found the treasure, he would have purchased a large hacienda and probably would have lost everything in the Revolution and died poor. *¿Quién sabe?*

The captain's ghost behaved as we expect ghosts to behave, as the malevolent protector of ill-gotten gains. He also did as expected by staying put. Ghosts are generally associated with a place; witness the classic haunted house. But a ghost may have occupied a place since long before anything was built there, for so long that the reason for the ghost's presence is lost to us. Cyrus Morton told me such a story.

Cyrus was a Gullah from the Georgia Sea Islands who had never lived on the mainland. When I met him he was eighty and living on Ossabaw Island. He was more or less retired then, doing a little gardening, a little fishing, and just keeping an eye on things, all sorts of things.

I met Cyrus while I was at the artists' colony there, back about 1980. I came back to listen to him tell stories and to try to record some of them. Cyrus had been on the island more than sixty years by then. He was one of the best naturalists I've ever met, for he didn't place limits on what his mind could accept. He observed everything and tried to fit it all together into a natural pattern. The result was immense knowledge of the island and the waters around it. And a tremendous hoard of stories that he would share at the right time.

One day, as I was passing Middle Place, heading to South End, Cyrus was coming out of the marsh below Middle Place, carrying a basket of crabs. People had been crabbing there for time out of mind, and occasionally someone still picked up Indian artifacts around Middle Place; there had been villages there long before the first plantation was built. Where we stopped to visit, we could see the remains of a small cabin, overgrown and melting back into the forest. It was one of many structures that had occupied the site in the last few thousand years. But I knew there was a story associated with that particular cabin, so I pointed to it and asked Cyrus why it faced back into the woods rather than into the Middle Place clearing. Cyrus set his basket of crabs down and leaned on his walking stick. I leaned back against a tree and listened.

Back in the 1920s, before Sandy West's family bought the island, Ossabaw was a hunting club, owned by a group of wealthy New Yorkers. They came down several times a year to hunt and fish. The rest of the time the island was left alone, pretty much as wild as when the Spanish first sailed past it. Cyrus and his brother worked there, growing a little corn, taking care of the dogs, building hunting blinds, repairing boats, and the host of other chores needed to make the place work. When the owners came down, Cyrus and his brother were guides and boatmen; they set decoys, caught bait, cleaned and butchered the kill, and so on.

One summer, while things were quiet, Cyrus and his brother built the cabin at Middle Place, facing out into the clearing of the earlier plantation house that had burned down before Cyrus's days on the island. The one-room cabin sat at the edge of the clearing, facing out into the opening, with the marsh fifty yards off to the south. They built the cabin, but didn't stay in it until hunting season.

The owners were coming for a duck hunt, and Cyrus needed to set out decoys at the Middle Place marsh. He started late and planned to spend the night in the new cabin, taking with him bedding, kitchen utensils, and groceries as well as the decoys. It took all afternoon to set the decoys and check the blinds, so it was becoming dark and getting cold when he finished. He parked the wagon at the door of the cabin and picketed the mules to graze in the clearing.

After getting his bedding on the cot and the food and utensils in the cabinets, Cyrus built a fire in the small stove. He left the door open on the little wood-burner so that he didn't need to light the lantern. After supper, Cyrus sat, watched the flames, and thought his thoughts until his eyes grew heavy. He pulled off his boots and crossed to the bed. As he stood at the edge of the cot, turning his bedding down, a hand reached out from under it and grabbed Cyrus by the ankle.

Cyrus was not a big man, but he was powerfully built and uncommonly strong. He thought his brother had sneaked in and was trying to scare him. So he reached down and grabbed the wrist and twisted the hand free from his ankle, and then jerked. He almost fell, because he was expecting the weight of his brother. Instead of his brother, what Cyrus jerked out from under the bed was a hand and arm that ended just below the elbow. The hand opened and closed, grasping as though still trying to grab him.

Cyrus did what most of us would have done: he dropped the hand. It hit the floor and scuttled back under the bed. Then Cyrus did something that I think few people would have done. Instead of running, he stepped to the door and retrieved his shotgun from the wagon, all the while keeping an eye on the room. He then closed and latched the door, lit the lantern, and searched the cabin. The search didn't take long. The only furniture in the cabin other than the stove and the bed was a table and a couple of chairs. The cabinets and shelves were open boxes nailed to the walls, five feet up. Cyrus ransacked the bed, taking all the bedding off and shaking it out. The hand wasn't there, or anywhere else in the cabin. And there was no way for the hand to come in or go out; the windows were closed and the door latched. Cyrus closed the door and the damper on the stove, collected his bedding, and slept in the wagon that night.

When Cyrus told his brother the next morning, he laughed and told Cyrus it was simply a nightmare.

Cyrus pointed out that it had happened before he went to bed, not after. But his brother just laughed at Cyrus for sleeping outside in the cold when there was a warm stove just a few feet away. Cyrus shut up and waited.

In a couple of weeks there was another hunt scheduled for the marsh at Middle Place. Someone had to go down the day before and set out decoys and check on the blinds. Cyrus refused to go, so his brother went, laughing about Cyrus being afraid of his dreams. His brother figured Cyrus would sneak down and try some prank. He was prepared for trouble.

The weather had turned warm, so, after he had cooked his supper, he let the fire burn out. But he lit the lantern and brought the shotgun inside. He checked carefully under the bed, and anywhere the hand—or Cyrus—could hide. Satisfied that he was alone, he retired, putting his shotgun next to him on the bed before blowing out the lantern.

No sooner had he lain down than the bed began to rock and bounce. He figured Cyrus had somehow rigged the bed so that he could shake it from outside. Figuring to turn the tables on Cyrus, he leaped from bed, shotgun in hand. He figured a couple of shots into the air, from the door, would scare Cyrus off. When he hit the floor he realized it wasn't the bed that was shaking, but the whole cabin. He knew Cyrus was strong, but not that strong. He was knocked off his feet before he reached the door. He clung to the floor as the cabin began to spin. It spun completely around several times before coming to rest, off the blocks and facing the opposite direction. When it stopped, he bolted from the cabin. It's only about four miles back up to where they lived, at North End. He spent the night there. The next day, in broad daylight, the brothers collected everything from the cabin.

Cyrus told me that no one had slept in the cabin since. He speculated that maybe there was an old Indian graveyard under the cabin, and the spirits there didn't like someone sleeping above them.

We looked through the woods at the remains of the cabin. It sagged as though tired of standing, ready to fall down and rejoin the forest. Cyrus looked over at me and said, "You could spend the night in there if you wanted to." But I figured some stories were better left mysterious.

The classic haunted house is a rambling, rundown mansion. Sheridan, Wyoming, can't boast such a house, but it does contain a certain wonderful old haunted hotel. There is no mystery about who haunts the Sheridan Inn, though; everyone knows Miss Kate. And everyone knows that Miss Kate is still at the Inn because she loves it.

Buffalo Bill built the Sheridan Inn across the street from the new train depot in the 1890s. It was considered the finest hotel between Chicago and Seattle, occupying, with its grounds, an entire block. A porch extends along the front and two sides of the building, and the roofline is broken by sixty-nine gables to give light to the upstairs rooms. Inside the front doors is a gracious lobby with oak wainscoting and pine beams setting off a cobblestone fireplace. A stairway leads up to the rooms, and hallways lead to the dining room and saloon. The dining room has woodwork and a fireplace to match the lobby. The saloon is set off by a magnificent oak bar and back-bar imported from England.

Buffalo Bill used to sit on the porch to audition acts for his Wild West Show; bucking horses tearing up the front lawn as bronc stompers showed their stuff. Today the cottonwoods have grown too large for bronc riding on the lawn. There are no passenger trains unloading tired and hungry people across the street. The Interstate is a mile and a half to the east. It is quiet under the shade of the cottonwoods now, the quiet of the old days remembered. But in the old days it was a bustling place, too. The Inn had its own generator for lights, and the first phone line in town, a direct link to the drugstore so that weary travelers could order anything they might need. It was in those bustling days just before the turn of the century that Miss Kate Arnold arrived at the Inn.

Miss Kate came to Sheridan to get married. Her fiancé wasn't at the train station, or anywhere else to be seen, so she crossed the street and took a room at the Inn. By the time she persuaded herself that he wasn't coming (neither Miss Kate nor anyone else in Sheridan ever knew what happened to him), she didn't have enough money to go home. She took a job at the Inn to make enough money to go home, not realizing she was already home. Miss Kate lived and worked at the Inn for over sixty years.

The Inn has been blessed with many people who

care for it, fall in love with it, and help it to survive. In the 1960s, Neltje stepped in and bought it, sight unseen, to keep it from being torn down. In the following months, Neltje and Miss Kate became friends. Neltje offered to let Miss Kate stay in her room the rest of her life, but Miss Kate moved to a retirement home. As she told Neltje, she was getting forgetful and she knew, having installed it herself, how old and worn the wiring was in the Inn. She didn't want to burn down the place she loved.

After her death, Miss Kate was cremated and Neltje had her ashes placed inside the walls of her old room. More than Miss Kate's ashes remained in the hotel. In short order, Neltje realized that Miss Kate's ghost had moved into the Inn and was still actively involved in taking care of it. Neltje said she could always tell when Miss Kate was upset because she would rearrange the furniture in her room. Once she even rearranged it in the dining room.

The hotel was closed in those days; only the bar and restaurant were open, and those not until noon. The staff decided that it would be much easier to set the tables for dinner after they cleaned up from supper. Then the place would be ready when they came to work in the morning. One of the older employees told Neltje that Miss Kate had never allowed that when she was managing the place, but Neltje said she could see nothing wrong with the idea, and told the staff to go ahead.

On the first morning of the new system, the staff found, at each place setting, the silverware wrapped in the napkin and placed in the water glass.

Everyone thought it was a practical joke, laughed about it, and reset the tables. But Neltje was a bit nervous that someone had been able to get in so easily. The next night she carefully locked the doors and took the keys with her. The following morning the silverware and napkins were again in the water glasses, and the vase in Miss Kate's room was turned over. From then on the staff followed the old system without complaints.

On another occasion, one of the waitresses had her hand in the till. Not a living soul suspected anything was amiss. But Miss Kate had kept the Inn's books for years, and was evidently still keeping her eyes on the accounts. The Inn used large round pewter trays for serving, the sort that are best carried balanced on the palm above the waitress's shoulder. One night the sticky-fingered waitress was gliding gracefully across the dining room floor with a heavily laden tray above her head. A number of witnesses, several of them old enough to remember Miss Kate personally, all of them knowing of her continued presence at the Inn, saw the waitress's ponytail seized and jerked backward, though no one was anywhere near her. The jerk pulled her back hard enough to throw her. She screamed in pain and fell; tray and dishes clattered to the floor.

The waitress got the message and quit. Several weeks later the Inn's accountant found the evidence of the waitress's pilferage. Miss Kate had saved the Inn far more than the cost of the dishes she broke that night.

Neltje gave the Inn to the Denver Children's

Hospital a few years ago. The bust of the late eighties came soon afterwards, and hard economic times
forced the hospital to close it up. The people of
Sheridan bought it and operate it now as a museum,
hoping to be able to reopen the restaurant and
saloon in the not-too-distant future. And, of course,
everyone hopes that someday the hotel itself can be
renovated. If it is, I hope and suspect that one room
will stay as it has been for years. For I am sure that
Miss Kate still watches over it as she has since that
day she arrived in Sheridan, thinking she was coming to meet a man rather than her dream.

Some spirits are so closely tied to places or events
that they remain, long after their bodies have left.
There are ghosts that survive in our imaginations
because we need them. And there are stories of
ghosts that seem to be essential to our psyches. I
promise that if you take the time to listen, you will
hear some. Some will be scary, some mysterious,
some delightful, many hard to believe. But do not
dismiss them out of hand, for you never know when
you might awaken to find a ghost, just passing
through.

AMERICAN
FOLKTALES

∧.∧.∨.∧.∧

One evening this past January I found myself telling stories to a group of students at Marrick Priory in Swaledale, North Yorkshire, England. The priory was abandoned in the 1530s or 1540s and stands now as a ruin, save for the chapel, where we sat that early evening. In the unsure light and shadow of twilight, I sensed the reach of time, the light and shadow of history and folk belief, stretching back to the building of the priory, nearly four hundred years before Columbus sailed. I felt the shallowness of our American cultural roots. As night drew on, I went outside to see the stars through the broken clouds and reflected that, while the English use the deep-rooted oak as a symbol of their land and

culture, we in the American West use the tumble-
weed, a plant that not only gives up its roots to spread
its seeds, but is not even native. The English oak has
cultural ties dating back to the Druids; the tumble-
weed came with immigrant farmers.

Eight months later, I was telling stories while sitting in the shadows of Spruce Tree House, an
Anasazi cliff dwelling at Mesa Verde. As I talked, the
deep shadows, fading into darkness at the back of
the cave, had an effect similar to the twilight at
Marrick Priory. I realized the stone walls there were
the same age as the ones at Marrick. And the people
who lived here told stories of the lives and times of
themselves and their ancestors, as did the people at
Marrick. The history and folklore of America are, I
know, as ancient as those of any other part of the
world. And they are my tales, since I too grew from
this soil. As an Englishman can honestly claim
Merlin as his cultural ancestor, even if all his ancestors arrived long after the Celtic period, so I claim
all the tales grown from the soil of my home country.

Here are a couple of American folktales, tales
grown from the land and passed on, through the
telling, from generation to generation. The first is an
ancient story. I've heard versions from three Indian
tribes, but there are many more from all over North
America and Siberia. I have borrowed from several
versions to tell the story of the Bear Mother:

In those long-ago days when the world was no
longer brand-new, but not yet old enough for people
to have been everywhere in it, there was a village. It

was small, made of earth, and sod-covered, so that you might not have seen it as you passed, unless people were outside or smoke curled noticeably from the holes in the tops of the huts. The small huts of each family and the larger communal hearth lodge could easily be mistaken for hillocks. The village did not look special; indeed, it looked much like the villages to the east, south, and west of it. But it was special because there were no villages to the north of it. To the north were only the wastelands, where no people could live because of Winter. The people of the village, like all people, had come from the south, where it is always spring, when new growth comes. It is also always fall there, when fruits ripen. In other words, there is always something to eat. But here, in this new land, Winter, the white giant of the north, came to visit each year, making a time of cold and starvation. If the people had not had such a good relationship with fire, they could not have survived. The central building of the village, the communal hearth, was where the fire spirit lived and was constantly tended. But even in summer, times weren't necessarily easy, for the plants that grew in this land were new to the people. No one knew how or when to harvest them, or how to use them for food or medicine. The people of the village knew that they could not return to the south because all the good lands there were already occupied. So the people of the village struggled to survive, and each year people died because there wasn't enough to eat. And there was no one to teach them the secrets of this new land.

One spring morning—not the spring of green grass, flowers, and butterflies, but early spring, the season of mud, when the snow is melting and the ground is thawing—a young woman was out picking berries. You can imagine how hard it is to pick berries in the spring, for berries ripen in the fall. The only berries left on the bushes were those that no one had picked the fall before, and that no bird could reach during the winter. They had been frozen and thawed a few times by spring, and looked more like raisins than berries. They weren't very good to eat, but better than the twigs they grew on, and one of the few foods the people of her village knew, so she was picking berries. It was hard work since the only berries left were in the center of the bushes, but if she worked hard from dawn to dusk, she might be able to fill her basket half full; if all the women of the village did as well, they would survive until the animals returned from wherever it was that so many disappeared to each winter.

As she crawled through the berry patch that morning, a shadow fell over her. When she looked up to see what was casting the shadow, she looked into the eyes of the most incredible man she had ever seen. He was tall and broad-shouldered. The leather his clothes were made of was better tanned than her peoples'. The stitching of the seams was finer. And the quill work was exquisite. The weapons he carried, while similar in design to those the men of her village carried, were far better made than any she had seen before. Besides, he was the most handsome man she had ever laid eyes on. He smiled at her, and it was like the sun coming out from behind a cloud on a spring day; it lit everything with hope and promise. Then he spoke to her. He told her that he had watched her from a distance for some time, and that he would like for her to come with him and marry him. She was a dutiful daughter and member of her village, and knew that she couldn't just run off with anyone who asked her to. But she was also able to see into her own heart and to know herself. She thought it over for three or four seconds and knew that she loved him. She said yes.

He helped her to her feet and they left together, walking toward his home. They walked all day to the north. This amazed her, for she knew that her village was as far north as any in the world. Yet, as the sun touched the horizon that evening, they came over a ridge into a beautiful valley. Through the center of the valley a river flowed. Beyond it hills, clad in the darkness of pines, stairstepped back to mountains piled deep with snow. But her vision was held by the lodge set near the river, and the people returning to it in the last light of day. The lodge was similar in design to the lodges of her people, but it was as big as her whole village. Smoke rose from several smoke holes down its length. The young woman could see people returning to the lodge from up and down the river. They were tall, handsome people, but, more than that, she saw that the women's baskets were full of food and the hunters were carrying game.

She walked with her husband-to-be down the hill and across the valley to his lodge, feeling that she had made a very wise decision to come with him.

Everyone else had gone inside when they arrived at the lodge, for dusk was deepening into night. Before they entered, her husband-to-be stopped her and said, "When we go inside, you must be very, very brave." Not knowing what he meant, she stooped and passed through the doorway. Inside, the young woman's eyes took a few moments to adjust from the darkness to the light of several hearth fires throwing strange shadows on the walls. She thought how strange it was that, in spite of the fires, everyone had kept on his coat or robe, for the shadows all seemed hairy. As her eyes became accustomed to the light, though, she realized that the people had not only taken off their robes but their skins as well. They were all grizzly bears.

The young woman eased back toward the door, intent on escape from this lodge of bears, when her husband-to-be put his hand on her shoulder, stopped her, and said, "Listen." When she stopped the pounding of her heart long enough to do so, she realized that she could understand the language of the bears. More important, she realized that she understood what they were talking about. For they spoke of the things her people (or, for that matter, any people, then or now) would be talking about as they waited for supper to cook. They were talking about where they had been that day and what they had done, where they were going tomorrow, the things they had seen and thought of. They were laughing quietly and telling jokes and stories. Hearing this, the young woman knew she was safe there. As she turned to tell her husband-to-be that she felt safe, she was shocked to see him taking off his human skin; she realized that he too was a grizzly bear. The future of our species hung in the air between their eyes. Had the young woman been any less sure of her heart or any less brave, she would have fled and we would have lost...well, you will see what we would have lost. But her love and her bravery won the moment and both the woman and the bear man knew it. He took her into the lodge and introduced her. The bear people made her welcome.

That night she had something she had never before had at that time of the year: enough to eat for supper. Not only was the food plentiful, it was delicious, even though she had no idea what most of it was. After supper the bear people sat up late, telling stories and singing. The young woman had had a long day; she grew tired before the singers did, and was given a bed of her own. She fell asleep to the sound of singing and drums that beat with the rhythm of the earth's heartbeat. The next morning was like waking from a dream into a dream. The young woman lay for a time, wrapped in her robes, enjoying her dreams of the bear people and the smell of breakfast cooking. Suddenly she sat bolt upright, realizing that the smell was real and the dream was not a dream; she was in the bear lodge and breakfast was cooking. She had never before, in the spring of the year, had breakfast. But here, in the bear lodge, there was so much food that after everyone had eaten his fill at supper the night before, there was plenty left over for breakfast. She wondered how they could have so much more than her people.

She did not have to wonder for long. After they had finished eating, the bear people went outside, pausing to put on their human skins at the door. Outside, the bear women took the young woman with them and began to teach her. What they taught her were the songs of plants. For, she learned, each plant has a song; if you learn it, then you know when to harvest a plant, how to harvest it, what part to use for food, medicine, dye, cordage, and so on. Most important, the song told the plant that the bear people honored and respected it so that it would not hurt them and would grow there again.

All through the spring, summer, and fall she stayed with the bear people, learning plant songs, getting to know the bear people in general and her husband-to-be in particular. But, as fall drew on toward winter, she became homesick. She had not seen her family and old friends for almost as many moons as she had fingers, and she missed them. When she told her husband-to-be how she felt, he looked down at her and smiled, saying, "I think you should go. Spend the winter in your parents' village. If, in the spring, you find you still love me, come back. The only thing I ask is that you tell no one of me and my people, of this place, or of how you learned all you have to teach." She agreed readily, and prepared to go visit her family and friends.

The day she left, the bears loaded her down with gifts to take back to her village. When she arrived there, the people were amazed. She had disappeared without a trace, and had been gone for the better part of a year. Everyone had given her up for dead.

Now she was back and carrying rich gifts. The next day people realized the greatest gift she had brought. For it was then she began to teach the people the plant songs she had learned from the bear people. It was a gift they treasured, for it meant that they could not only survive but prosper in this new land.

So the winter passed. Of course, some of her friends asked where she had lived and who had taught her, but she was able to change the conversation and not tell them. On the whole, the people of her parents' village were so glad to learn the songs that they didn't care where they came from. When spring arrived and the young woman had taught all the songs she had learned that year, she found that she was homesick for the bear lodge, the bear people, and especially her husband-to-be. So one morning the people of the village awoke to find that the young woman had left during the night.

When she arrived at the bear lodge that evening, all the people in general and her husband-to-be in particular were glad of her return and welcomed her back to their hearth. And another year began with the greening of the spring. At the height of spring, when the world was most alive, the young woman and her bear man were married by the customs of the bear lodge. And that spring, summer, and fall were as wonderful as can be imagined. Some days the young woman went out with the bear women to learn plant songs. Other days she went out with the bear men to learn the songs of animals and the hunt. And at night the bear people, men and women together, taught her the songs of love and joy, the epic tales, and the laughter that made their lives rich beyond measure.

As fall drew toward winter, though, she began to feel homesick for her human family and friends. She told her husband what she was feeling, and he smiled his smile at her and said, "I think you should go to your parents' village for the winter. If, in the spring, you still love me, come back. The only thing I ask is that you tell no one of me and my people, of this place, or of how you've learned all you have to teach." She agreed, and left the next day to visit her family, carrying many gifts from the bear people. The people of her village weren't surprised by her return that year. They were, however, excited, for they expected her to arrive with gifts and more songs. They had food stored for the winter, thanks to what the young woman had taught them the winter before. But they had also had time to wonder and talk about how and where she had learned so much. Their curiosity had become stronger than their manners. Before the young woman had set done her bundle of gifts, the people began to ask her where she was living and whom she had married. She laughed and told them she was too tired to talk that night. But she went to bed worried about the reception and woke to find her worries justified; that day, and every day following, people asked her the same questions. Finally she called all the village together and told them that where she lived and who her teachers were was a secret that she could not reveal. She said that they must trust her and have respect for her wishes. But their curiosity was so great that

they continued to ask her and even to try to trick her
into telling her secret. She continued to teach them
only because they weren't able to question her while
she was teaching them songs. It was the longest,
most miserable winter of her life. As soon as the
snow was off the land enough for her to travel, she
left her parents' village and returned to the bear
lodge. Her husband and all the other bear people
were so happy to have her back that she realized the
bear lodge was her real home and the bear people
her real family. As she and her husband lay snuggled
deep in their sleeping robes that night, she knew that
she would never return to her parents' village.

That year, spring was a joy that gave way to a rich
summer that in its turn yielded to a fall filled with
the ripe rewards of a perfect year. All through the
three seasons the young woman had learned and
shared with the bear people and become, in her
spirit and in theirs, a part of the bear lodge. That
time of the fall came when, in the two years past, the
young woman had felt homesick for her old village.
This year she felt nothing but the peace and happiness of the bear lodge. She told her husband that she
wanted to stay with him at the bear lodge that winter. He smiled, and it had the effect it always had—
that of the sun returning after a storm—but when he
spoke, he told her, "This winter you can't stay here.
You do not know all the plant songs yet. Not until
you have learned all of them can we teach you our
greatest magic, our winter magic. By this time next
year you will know them all, and then, if you want,
we will teach you the winter magic and you will be

fully a part of the bear lodge. But this winter you have to go back to your old village. If, in the spring, you still love me, come back. And again I must ask you not to tell anyone whom you have married or where you are living."

So again she returned to her old village for the winter, and it was worse than the last had been. The people questioned her and tried to trick her every day. Her only way of avoiding the questions was by teaching people the songs she had learned that year, for while the people were learning the songs, they couldn't ask her the songs' origins. The winter dragged on, seemingly without end, and each day the young woman grew to dislike and distrust the people of her parents' village even more because they refused to honor her requests for privacy. She knew in her heart, even before the sun turned back to the north, that when the snows had melted and she had returned to the bear lodge, she would never set foot in the village again. Snow was still drifted deep in the draws and sheltered places when she headed home to the bear lodge. With each pace away from the village, her step was lighter and she felt the freedom of her future. By the evening, when she crossed the ridge and looked down into the valley of the bear lodge, her joy brought tears to her eyes. As she hurried down the slope, the bear people returning to the lodge saw her and sang out happily. She broke into a run to reach them, laughing and crying at the same time.

But this time there were witnesses to the reunion. The previous fall, before the young woman arrived there, everyone in her parents' village had met and decided that if she didn't tell them where she was living and how she was learning all the songs, the three best hunters in the village would follow her in the spring. Now it happened that the three best hunters in the village were her brothers. They were such good hunters that the young woman didn't know she was being followed. As she ran to meet the bear people at the lodge, her brothers hid and watched from the same spot where she had first seen the bear lodge three springs earlier. They saw the joy of the meeting, saw the happiness of their sister. They also saw the bear lodge, a single lodge as big as their whole village. And they saw the people, the women as big as the brothers; the men were bigger, much bigger. In whispered tones they discussed what might happen if they were discovered. The men did not look like the sort the brothers wanted to pick a fight with. The brothers decided that they would stay hidden on the ridge until after dark and then slip away and return home. They would tell everyone that their sister had married a good man, and leave it at that.

There was a beautiful sunset that evening, and one old man stayed outside the bear lodge to watch it. In the twilight, as the colors faded from the western sky and night rose in the east, the old man took off his human skin before going into the lodge. The brothers watched in stunned amazement. When they finally found their voices again, they discussed the meaning of what they had seen, and decided that everyone in the lodge must be a bear and that their sister was bewitched. Had they not been her brothers, perhaps they would still have returned home and said nothing. If they had left, how different would our lives be today? Humans and bears might have become friends over time. Our whole relationship with the animal world might be different. But since it was their sister, the brothers felt they must rescue her.

Inside the bear lodge there was a party that evening. The bear people knew that the young woman had returned to stay. They celebrated because they loved her and welcomed her. There was plenty of food, laughter, and music in the bear lodge that night. It was bright, warm, and full of love. When the party ended and the bear people turned to their sleeping robes and the young woman's husband started to retrieve his human skin, she stopped him. Every night they had been together since they wed, he had put on his human skin at bedtime. But this night she stopped him, for, as she told him, she knew that she loved him for who he was in his heart, not for what he looked like. For the first time they slept together, she as a woman and he as a bear. And their sleeping robes were filled with love.

Outside the bear lodge, up on the ridge, the brothers made their preparations to save their sister, and waited. Finally, in the dead part of the night, halfway between midnight and dawn, when everything and everyone sleeps, the brothers slipped down off the ridge, and crept inside the lodge. The hearths glowed faintly, allowing, in their meager light, the brothers to see all the bears, dark mounds in their sleeping robes, and their sister's pale face and shoulder. Quietly the brothers slipped from sleeping robe to sleeping robe and, with spears and knives, silently killed all the bear people.

When they woke their sister to tell her that she had been rescued, she found her husband's blood on her. The joy she had felt that evening was replaced with grief that never could be healed. Her brothers had killed her husband and his family, her family. She didn't want to leave the bear lodge, but her brothers burned the lodge and forced her to return with them to their village. She lived there the rest of her life, though she never forgave the people, for they never acknowledged or understood their crime. Here the story would have ended, and quite possibly our time in the north lands would have ended not long after that, but for one thing. Nine months after her return, the young woman gave birth to twin sons.

The sons were not like other children. They were shape-shifters and could be either human or grizzly bear as they chose. They were strangers in their own village, neither accepted nor accepting. Their mother, now properly called the Bear Mother, taught them the story of how their father and his family, their kin, had been killed. She also taught them the songs she had learned from the bear people. As soon as they were old enough, the Bear Sons left the village and traveled around the world, slaying monsters, teaching people the songs of plants, and helping to form the northern world's cultures. There are myriad stories of the Bear Sons and their deeds, for they were the first heroes; but these are other stories for other times.

It is important to remember that the Bear Mother did not learn all the plant songs. There are plants that bears, knowing the songs, can eat, but that we must avoid. And of course we never learned the bears' greatest magic, the winter magic that allows them to dig a hole and bury themselves in the fall and rise again from underground when spring arrives. And if you are ever around grizzly bears, you should remember that every bear learns the story of the Bear Mother when it is a young cub. Unless you know how a particular bear feels about the story, it is a good idea not to get too close, because some of them still blame us for what happened that last night at the bear lodge.

The Trickster is found in myths and folktales around the world. In North America the character of the Trickster is often an animal. Probably the best known of these figures is Coyote. Coyote has, in the last few years, known a renaissance among nontraditional storytellers. His great power as the Trickster in many Indian myths has been recognized. Unfortunately, there has been, it seems, an emphasis placed on the comic aspects of that role. Most of the stories I encounter in print or repeated by storytellers are those in which Coyote gets into trouble through his tricks. I don't want to belittle those tales; they are real and important. But it is also important to remember that Coyote helped to create the world as we know it. He named everything, making it knowable. Yet, even when engaged in serious activity, Coyote never leaves his sense of humor behind. Life is good and fun. The problems he encounters, though they are real and serious on many occasions, he never attempts to avoid.

But enough talk about Coyote. He explains himself far better in his stories than anyone else can in talking about him. Before I go any further, I must tell you that whenever you hear a story begin, "Coyote was going along..." (which is how Coyote stories usually begin, just as fairy tales begin, "Once upon a time...") don't listen unless it is winter. Coyote stories are winter tales. As I write this, there is snow on the ground and stars in the sky. One of the problems of writing is that I have no control over when you read this. I must, however, warn you that it is a winter tale and I recommend that, if it is not now winter, you pass this story by and return to it on a quiet, cold night.

Coyote was going along, thinking about how much his chin hurt. His chin hurt because he had just stepped in a hole and fallen, banging his chin on a rock. He hadn't seen the hole because it was dark. It wasn't night. Well, it might have been night, you really couldn't tell because there wasn't any day or night; it was dark all the time. Animals could only find their way around by listening and smelling, and that hole hadn't smelled any different. So Coyote was walking and thinking. Suddenly, coming over a ridge, Coyote knew that there was a lodge in the distance. He stopped, puzzled, because he had heard nothing and he couldn't smell the lodge. How did he know it was there? He realized that those two things in the front of his head that he called eyes had some use. They allowed him to...he decided he would call it *see*, because there was...*light* would be a good word...leaking out from inside the lodge.

Coyote thought that if there was light outside that lodge, everyone could see and life would be much easier. He decided that he'd go to the lodge and see if whoever lived there would share some of the light. Coyote trotted down the slope and across the flat toward the lodge, his nose almost touching the ground, sniffing for holes and big rocks. When he arrived at the lodge, Coyote could tell by the size and smell that it belonged to a spirit. So Coyote drew himself up as tall and proud as he could and scratched on the wall of the lodge, next to the door.

"What do you want?" a voice boomed out, huge and angry. Coyote shrank back, but then stepped back up to the door and announced who he was and said, "I was wondering if you might be willing to share some of the light you have in your lodge with those of us out here?"

"No!"

"But—"

"No! Never!"

Coyote walked off, thinking. He thought about how to get some of that spirit's light for the rest of the world. Of course, being Coyote, he thought of a plan pretty quickly, and went sniffing around for Mouse to help him. When Coyote and Mouse returned to the spirit's lodge, Mouse was as fascinated with light and with seeing as Coyote had been, and was willing to help. So Coyote lifted the back edge of the lodge, and Mouse slipped in. Mouse hid behind a parfleche and then scurried over and got under a robe that was on the floor. He crept beneath it to the center of the lodge where the light was. Mouse seized a piece of the light and scampered back to the edge of the lodge, where he scratched on the wall. Outside, Coyote, crouching with his ear to the wall of the spirit's lodge, heard the faint scratching of Mouse and raised the edge of the lodge for him to slip out. As soon as he was outside, there was light, and Coyote and Mouse stood in awe at the view around them. But the spirit knew that some of the light had escaped or been stolen, and came roaring out of his lodge. Mouse had seen how big the spirit was, so he quickly tossed the light to Coyote and Coyote took off, running as fast as he could. Now Coyote is pretty fast, so Mouse was amazed at how quickly the spirit ran him down. But that was nothing compared to Mouse's amazement at what the spirit did to Coyote then. It kicked Coyote all over the prairie. It would kick him high into the sky and then kick him across the prairie when he came down. By the time Coyote had stopped rolling, the spirit would be there and kick him back toward the lodge or high into the sky again. When the spirit finally took his light and went back inside, Mouse went over to Coyote to see how he was doing.

"Are you all right, Coyote?" Mouse asked.

"Oh yes," Coyote replied. "It just broke all the bones in my body. I'll be fine." Then Coyote groaned and passed out. (If you aren't familiar with Coyote, having all his bones broken might seem serious, but Coyote is an immortal. In many of his stories he is killed and in a few days is again alive and well.)

In a few days Coyote was not only fully recovered, but was prepared to try again to steal light for the rest of the world. He called all the animals together, and from the ridge where he had first seen the spirit's lodge, he showed it to them. They all thought that the light would be a good thing to have in the world, so they agreed to help get it. Coyote explained that they could form a relay to outrun the spirit.

Coyote arranged the animals in order, from Antelope, the fastest, through Eagle, Deer, Hawk, Rabbit, and so on down to Turtle, the slowest. Each animal had set out the distance it could travel as fast as it could go. The next-slowest animal waited, at the end of that distance. Coyote explained that though the relay would be constantly slowing down, so would the spirit, and finally it would get too tired to continue the chase and give up. Then the animals would have light in the world and they would all be able to use their eyes.

Actually Turtle wasn't the last animal in line; Coyote was. He wasn't sure of the spirit, and he reasoned that if he had figured wrong and the spirit could keep up the pace, the last in line was least likely to be the one kicked around—especially with Turtle in front of him.

Having seen the spirit's strength and speed, Mouse did not volunteer to go back into the lodge. He figured the spirit would expect another attempt to steal the light. He didn't want to tangle with the spirit; Mouse was not immortal. Spider had volunteered. She did not, however, plan to go under the lodge wall as Mouse had done. Spider climbed up the outside of the lodge and lowered herself through the smoke hole by one of her silken threads. As she expected, the spirit was watching for a small animal to sneak in, but it was watching the floor, not the ceiling. Spider grabbed a small piece of the light and climbed back up her thread until she was above the spirit's head. There she stopped and spun a ball of her webbing around the light, trying to cover it completely so that no light could leak out. She had listened to both Coyote's and Mouse's versions of the story of the first attempt to steal light, and knew that the spirit had known when the light was outside, but she thought that if the light was covered, the spirit might not know it was gone. Spider was right, as she usually is. Unfortunately, it is almost impossible to tell if you have completely covered light in a lighted place. When she crawled back up her thread and out through the smoke hole, she realized that she had missed a single strand of webbing, and a thin beam of light leaked out of the ball. Spider heard the roar of the spirit as the light shone out of the ball. She raced down the side of the lodge and tossed the ball to Antelope just as the spirit emerged from the lodge. Antelope raced across the prairie as only antelope can, yet the spirit was grabbing at his tail from start to finish. Eagle fared no better, actually losing two tailfeathers to the spirit before she could pass the ball on. And so the race went.

Coyote was half right. The spirit did slow down, but at the same rate the animals did. It didn't stop, though. By the time the ball got to Turtle, the spirit was only a step or two behind. Coyote was surprised to see, in the dim glow of Spider's ball, that the spirit was still in the chase. Coyote did breathe a sigh of relief, though. As slow as Turtle was, the spirit would catch him and Coyote wouldn't have to go through another kicking. The spirit might even break a toe on Turtle's shell. Coyote was in for a surprise. Turtle had made sure that his leg of the relay started at the top of a steep hill. When he got the ball, Turtle stuck it in his mouth, flipped up on the edge of his shell, pulled his head and legs into his shell, and rolled down the hill, faster than Coyote could have run down it. Turtle was dizzy when he got to Coyote, but he stuck his head out of his shell long enough to spit the ball to Coyote. Coyote ran as fast as he could, but there was no one to give the ball to; he had to keep running. The farther he ran, the slower he went. The spirit began to gain on him. Coyote's lungs ached and his legs were getting wobbly. He knew the spirit would catch him in another few jumps and Coyote didn't want to get kicked around again, so he took the ball from his mouth and threw it as high and as hard as he could, thinking that the spirit might go after the light rather than after him. Now, Coyote has quite an arm. He threw the ball so high and so hard that it hit the top of the sky and broke. Spider's web ball fell away, and the ball of light stuck in the middle of the sky. The spirit looked up at the light, then hung his head and walked back to his lodge, never to come out again.

All the animals gathered around Coyote, congratulating him and marveling at what he had done. It was light everywhere. (The ball of light in the center of the sky, which Coyote named the Sun, was so bright that none of the animals could look directly at it.) Within two weeks the back-slapping and congratulations had stopped. There was much muttering, and some animals were outspoken in their displeasure. It was light all the time. Animals were having trouble sleeping; when they tried, the sun shone in their eyes. Also, it seemed to be getting hotter as time passed. Coyote was muttering too, about how, no matter what you did for folks, they complained. Coyote was doing more than muttering; he was thinking, partially because he was worried that the other animals might take out their frustrations on him, and partially because he was having trouble sleeping himself, though he would never have admitted it. When Coyote starts thinking, something happens—not always something good, but something. This time was no different. Coyote went to every animal and had it give something of its power, a single hair from each mammal, a feather from each bird, and something that was part of each insect's character—a length of thread from Spider, a long blade of grass from Grasshopper, and so on. Taking all these, Coyote braided a very long, very strong rope. He tied a hondo in one end of the rope. Coiling the rope and building a loop, Coyote roped the sun and gave it a mighty jerk to the east, intending to pull the sun from the sky past the end of the earth.

Coyote didn't jerk it quite hard enough; the sun hit the edge of the earth and bounced back, breaking off many tiny pieces. The sun bounced back so hard that it crossed the sky and descended in the west. Coyote expected it to hit there and bounce back again, but it cleared the horizon and was gone, except for the tiny pieces that followed it more slowly. These tiny pieces gave some light, so that the animals could see a little bit. As soon as the sun was gone, the animals ran to congratulate Coyote. But within a few hours some were complaining. They realized that they preferred the light to the dark. Others were sure they preferred the dark. Coyote was muttering that no matter what you did for folks, they were never satisfied. Then, in a few hours, it started to get light in the east. In a little while the sun came back up and started across the sky again.

After the sun had come and gone a few times and all the animals knew that it would keep circling— that part of the time it would be light and part of the time dark—from then on, Coyote pretended that that was what he had planned all along. He announced that he had named the time when the sun was in the sky *day*, and that the time when it was gone and the little pieces he had broken off of it—which he had named *stars*—were in the sky *night*. The animals accepted that and so it has been, ever since. The animals that prefer the light, like Eagle or Turkey, are out during the day but asleep at night. Those animals that prefer the dark, like Owl or Mouse, sleep during the day and are active at night. There are, of course, some animals, like Deer, who have never been able to make up their minds, so, if you want to see them, you must look during the twilight, when the world is changing from day to night or night to day.

That is how the sun and stars, day and night got here. But, you are thinking, what about the moon? That is another story, for another time.

There are countless other examples of American myths, folktales, and legends. If we are ever to understand this land, we must someday learn its stories and put them in context with all the stories from cultures around the world that have arrived on these shores to contribute to our American culture. No matter what your heritage, these are your stories, for they are the stories of this land, our land, grown from our native soil.

In Conclusion

Oral literature is always a single generation away from extinction. Some of these stories might survive a bit longer, having been committed to print. But if you enjoyed one of these tales, please someday tell it to someone younger than you—someone who can, long after you are dead, tell it to someone else. The stories only live in the telling.

Index